When
Dragons
Dare to Dream

Praise for *When Dragons Dare to Dream*

'Jamie has done a brilliant job with this new book. It's a must-read for any football fan – I loved reading it, and I'm sure football fans will too.' JOE LEDLEY

'This really is a great book and I'd definitely recommend it to any football fan.' CHRIS GUNTER

'This superb book brings the best summer ever back to life in glorious technicolour. For those that were there, it's a chance to remember and reminisce. For those that weren't, it's an in-depth analysis of the what/where/when and the wonderful. Great passion – great insight. A must-have for all Welsh football fans.' DYLAN EBENEZER

Praise for *The Dragon Roars Again*

'An excellent contribution to Welsh football literature. I have met and spoken with Jamie on a number of occasions during the campaign and his support and enthusiasm for Welsh football is clear.' CHRIS COLEMAN

'A superbly researched book, full of in-depth information on Wales' return to the pinnacle of football from the people who made it possible. An incredible story, very well told.' ROGER SPEED

'A comprehensive and passion-filled account of what made qualification possible.' MARK PITMAN

When
Dragons
Dare to Dream

WALES' EXTRAORDINARY CAMPAIGN
AT THE EURO 2016 FINALS

JAMIE THOMAS

WITH FOREWORDS BY
JOE LEDLEY AND CHRIS GUNTER

First impression: 2016

© Copyright Jamie Thomas and Y Lolfa Cyf., 2016

The publishers wish to acknowledge the support of
Cyngor Llyfrau Cymru

Cover design: Y Lolfa
Front cover photograph: PA Images
Back cover photograph: David Rawcliffe (Propaganda Photo)
All other photographs: David Rawcliffe (Propaganda Photo)
& Jamie Thomas

ISBN: 978 1 78461 356 3

Published and printed in Wales
on paper from well-maintained forests by
Y Lolfa Cyf., Talybont, Ceredigion SY24 5HE
website www.ylolfa.com
e-mail ylolfa@ylolfa.com
tel 01970 832 304
fax 832 782

Contents

Author Acknowledgements

THE MORE I wrote of my first book, *The Dragon Roars Again*, the more convinced I became that I should quit while I was ahead and not publish it, because it wasn't good enough and guys like Chris Wathan and Bryn Law would put me to shame with their own versions. After it came out, I was equally certain I'd get bad reviews on Amazon and people tweeting, texting or calling me saying how wide of the mark it was, and how I'd missed this major point or that one.

I'm extremely relieved to say that none of that happened. Well, I did think the other books written were pretty superb, particularly Chris', but I was ecstatic with the reception my book received from everyone – whether that be people involved with the Wales squad on a day-to-day basis, fellow Wales fans, other journalists, or whoever.

In fact, one of the highlights of France for me was seeing a few people reading my book along the way and hearing that they enjoyed it, not knowing I was the author – a fact I kept to myself, just to be on the safe side! I must have done something right, and if you read no further into these acknowledgements I would like to say an enormous thank you, bigger than the one we gave our heroes upon their return to Cardiff on 8th July, to all of you who have bought, read, or even picked my first book up to have a look at it. Another big thank you goes to all the people who then reached out with positive messages about what was my first – and I thought would be my last – project of that nature. DIOLCH YN FAWR IAWN! It means so much to me, and I'll never forget any of it!

Whether this second book can live up to the standards of *The Dragon Roars Again*, I don't know, but I hope it can. If it is a success then it will be thanks in no small part to the excellent team at Y Lolfa, where Lefi Gruffudd and Carolyn Hodges have been instrumental in making this book what it is now.

I have to say a massive thank you to all of my friends for their incredible support throughout the process of writing this; whether it just be asking me how the book is going, or actually reading chapters for me and giving honest feedback. Owain, Anthony, Lauren, Rob and Ffion: thank you very much! Also, my favourite dweeb deserves a huge thank you for putting up with me disappearing to France for a month, then locking myself in a room for another five or six weeks afterwards to put this together – Laura, you're a special one... love you, mate! ;)

Of course, again, I couldn't have done this without the many fantastic individuals – players, fans, coaches, journalists – who gave me brilliant contributions and insights into their own unique journeys this past summer. Some of them were unfortunate enough to already have been pestered by me for *The Dragon Roars Again*, yet were still willing for me to interview them again for this latest book. Thank you very, very much to Chris Coleman, Ian Mitchell, Jack Collison, James Chester, Joe Ledley, Joey Jones, Jonathan Ford, Jonny Williams, Kit Symons, Neil Taylor, Owain Fôn Williams, Raymond Verheijen, Roger Speed, Sam Vokes, Mark Pitman, Dylan Ebenezer and Gary Pritchard for being so forthcoming and willing to have another sit-down with me about this incredible summer – I appreciate it beyond measure! I'm also incredibly grateful to the new contributors, of whom there are a few, for all of their time, support, kind words about the first book, and willingness to answer numerous questions for this latest effort. Chris Gunter, Michael O'Neill, Ian Gwyn Hughes, Rob Dowling, Mark Evans, Owain Tudur Jones, Barry Horne, Andrew Gwilym and Dylan Llewelyn: diolch yn fawr iawn, hogiau!

Finally, my thanks go to you, the readers, for giving my work a chance. The fact that you've taken the time to read a book (or two) by a guy in his early twenties with very little experience or reputation in this field, just a passion for the subject that it's obvious we all share, means more to me than I can actually put into words. Thank you.

Jamie Thomas
September 2016

Forewords

QUALIFICATION FOR EURO 2016 meant absolutely everything to us, as a team, as a nation of people who have waited our whole lives to see Wales competing at a major tournament. That feeling of qualifying was just amazing, and we couldn't wait to get to France to put our country on the map and make a nation proud of us once more.

So much was written about our journey to France – by our amazing fans on Twitter or online, by journalists in the papers and of course there were a few books written on Wales' qualification journey. Jamie's first book, *The Dragon Roars Again*, was one of those accounts of our country's journey. I read it whilst recovering from my fractured fibula in the build-up to the Euros, and I really enjoyed it. It's a top-quality book that tells the story this country has been on over the last few years in great detail, and does a fantastic job of telling readers exactly what qualifying for France meant for the whole of Wales.

We as players didn't want to go to France and come back with any regrets, however far we progressed into the tournament, and neither did the fans, nor anyone in a Welsh shirt. We players had the time of our lives – every single day was a pleasure, and I like to think the fans enjoyed it just as much as we did; we just didn't want it to end! To try and tell our nation's incredible story over the summer is no easy task, but Jamie's done a brilliant job of it with this new book. It's a must-read for any football fan – I loved reading it and I'm sure football fans will too!

JOE LEDLEY

MANY BOOKS WERE WRITTEN after the Euro 2016 qualifying campaign about the journey Wales had been on as a team, as a nation, to get to the point where we'd all seen a dream realised as Wales qualified for a major tournament.

Among those excellent books was Jamie's first title, *The Dragon Roars Again*, which told the story of Wales' journey over the last few years. His book really captured the emotion of it and was a very good, well-researched account of the journey of the players, the fans and the entire country as we all chased that dream of seeing Wales playing in a major competition.

I was very happy to hear that Jamie would be releasing another book, on the amazing experience we all shared at this summer's tournament, and I'm very pleased to say that this is another very good book that tells Wales' incredible story from the perspective of so many people who were involved: players, coaches, fans, journalists, everyone. This really is a great book and I'd definitely recommend it to any football fan!

CHRIS GUNTER

'It was everything I could have imagined and more, to be honest – more so just because of the special group of players I did it with, and the staff.'

NEIL TAYLOR, WALES INTERNATIONAL, 2010–

CHAPTER 1

After 58 years, just six months of waiting remained

'Chris was a little bit down after Sweden,
but the result didn't matter. I honestly felt that,
and he soon came around and agreed with me.'

KIT SYMONS, WALES NATIONAL TEAM COACH

THE GAME NEVER stops, we know that. Between the whistles is when the action takes place on the pitch in front of millions, but there are always training sessions, press conferences, interviews, Twitter debates, fans expecting things, etc etc – it's relentless! All of those things stepped up to another level for Wales in the months between qualifying and taking to the pitch in France for the first game of the tournament – though no more than people's expectations. OK, now Wales were a nation that had qualified for a tournament, but they were going to be expected to go out there and play in a way that reflected that: without weakness, without excuses, without second chances. 'It's something that we could sort of feel within the camp, I suppose,' said the team's Performance Psychologist,

Ian Mitchell. 'Once you've qualified there's a different sort of perception in terms of what needs to be done. I always talk to Chris about the importance of how we frame success, because once you've had success then complacency is never far behind. That's not saying that we did become complacent, just that we were aware of the dangers of complacency once we'd qualified, so we needed to frame our work as coaches in terms of how we manage individuals and the groups. Yes, there was a difference in perception once we'd qualified. There was relief because we'd got over the line, and there was always a danger of that sort of mindset creeping in about missing out right at the end, with the pressure perhaps beginning to tell towards the end of the campaign, so leading into the friendlies they were going to be difficult anyway.'

The 3–2 friendly defeat to the Netherlands at Cardiff City Stadium in November 2015, a month after qualification, proved an interesting test for Chris Coleman's men in the absence of their attacking triumvirate, Gareth Bale, Aaron Ramsey and Hal Robson-Kanu. On top of that, James Chester wasn't playing regularly for West Brom and nor was Joe Allen for Liverpool; Ashley Williams and Neil Taylor were in the middle of a difficult season for Swansea City, battling relegation; and Tom Lawrence was given the chance to lead the line for Wales on his own. Many looked at Holland, who hadn't qualified for the Euros, and basically rolled their eyes, thinking the likes of

Arjen Robben and co. wouldn't pose much of a threat because of their qualification struggles.

That was a ridiculous way of looking at things, and so it proved as Robben himself snatched a double and Bas Dost scored the other. Joe Ledley and Emyr Huws scored the goals for Wales, with the latter proving to be particularly impressive during the run of friendly fixtures leading up to the squad announcement in May. His teammate Jonny Williams was equally impressive throughout these games, and admitted that he had matured mentally over the previous year or so for Wales: 'Over the last year I've started to try and believe in myself a bit more – I'm not a 17-year-old kid anymore, I'm 22 now, nearly 23, so I've been told by a few people that I need to have more faith in myself and that this will help me on the pitch.' Joniesta went on to give particular praise to a manager who clearly has a lot of faith in the youngster: 'Chris Coleman always gives me that belief, that freedom to go and express myself and work hard, so I feel very comfortable in the Wales shirt, and I was able to do a good job in the friendlies.'

The highlight of the evening though, by far, was seeing Owain Fôn Williams win his first cap for Wales. This is a player who is as Welsh as they come, fiercely dedicated, and who had previously been included in over 30 Welsh squads before making his debut as a second-half substitute in this game. Fans were starting hashtags, tweeting the FAW, starting petitions, going all out to get this most loyal of footballers – a key part of the squad, thanks in no small part to his singing and his skills with a guitar – his first cap for the Welsh senior team. 'This is surely the highlight of my career. Nothing comes close to winning my first cap for my country and I don't think there will be a feeling that can top that throughout the rest of my career,' a jubilant Owain Fôn would note after the game. 'The fact that I'm part of a squad that has qualified for a major tournament – something this country hasn't achieved for nearly 60 years – it's an immense privilege to me to be a part of the whole thing. I've always said that if I wasn't part of the team then I would be in the stands cheering the guys on from the first minute to the last, but to actually be a part of the team is amazing for me.'

A few weeks later came the draw, and the question on everyone's lips was: would Wales be drawn against England? You could just see it coming – it seemed like fate that we'd be drawn together. Despite Wales being amongst the teams in Pot Four for the draw, and on that basis perceived as one of the lesser teams in the tournament, a certain top-seeded team didn't want to be drawn in the same group as Chris Coleman's Dragons, as the FAW's Rob Dowling recalled. 'Our Belgian counterparts came over to us to say how pleased they were that they hadn't drawn us in the group stages, because I think they see us as their bogey team.' Even though most of us weren't as lucky as Rob and had to be content with sitting at home watching history unfold before our eyes, he didn't hesitate to rub it in about how amazing an experience being at that draw was for the Welsh delegation, and summarised the occasion perfectly: 'That moment in Paris was one of the highlights of my career, and probably my life – it was a realisation, because suddenly you're there with all of the footballers and managers and superstars that you'd normally see when you're sat at home watching the television, so at that moment it's quite hard to take in because we're sat at the same table as all of these people. It was just surreal, in terms of all of the people you end up meeting and speaking to – I wouldn't say I was star-struck, it was just the feeling of being there amongst those people that you associate with major tournaments and success, so it felt really special to be a part of that.'

Drawing England is something Chris Coleman had said he wanted to avoid before the seemingly inevitable happened in Paris and Roy Hodgson's men were drawn against Wales, but on the other hand would anyone have preferred to play France, Germany, Spain, Belgium or Portugal? Better the devil you know, I say, and furthermore the run of fixtures worked perfectly for Wales too. With Slovakia and Russia also being drawn to face the Dragons, Chris Coleman's men would face the Slovaks first in Bordeaux, before meeting England in Lens and then taking on Russia in Toulouse to see out the group.

What better time to play England? Play them first and all of the pressure is on, with that crucial good start to the group on the line and the possible psychological effects of losing to your rivals hanging over you for the rest of the group stages. Play them last and everything rides on getting the right results in your first two games to avoid a crunch match in your final game. Play them second, and you have the perfect incentive to get off to a good start in the first game, then whether you win, lose or draw against England, you still have chance to respond in your final game with the memories of a strong first game to drive you forward. That's a very simple, somewhat optimistic, outlook of course, but with the new-found wave of positivity being surfed by the entirety of Welsh football, it was an outlook that a number of current and former players shared when I was speaking to them for various journalistic pieces in the build-up to the tournament.

One of the most important parts of the build-up, obviously, was the teams Wales chose to play against in their preparatory friendlies. It goes without saying that those opponents had to share certain similarities with the Dragons' eventual group opponents – not necessarily in terms of stature, but in terms of playing style and other characteristics such as their spirit and their followings both in the media and from supporters. Northern Ireland, Ukraine and Sweden were chosen as Wales' opponents, given that they bore particular resemblances to England, Slovakia and Russia respectively. Northern Ireland and England because of that 'British style of play and spirit'; Ukraine and Slovakia because of their strength in transition, as well as their counter-attacking style with wingers and number 10s who like to roam; and Sweden and Russia because of a mixture of all of those factors.

A clash with the Green and White Army came first, at the Cardiff City Stadium in March 2016, providing an opportunity for two of international football's greatest success stories in recent memory to come together and play a game of football on the way to the greatest summer of their lives. Chris Coleman's achievements as Wales manager have been incredible – I hope I made that infinitely clear in *The Dragon Roars Again* – but so have the achievements of Michael O'Neill and his Northern Ireland team. They qualified for Euro 2016 by topping their qualification group, finishing with an identical record to Wales of six wins, three draws and a solitary defeat.

The mutual admiration was clear between the two managers before the match, with Chris Coleman speaking glowingly of the Northern Ireland manager, and Michael O'Neill had this to say to the FAW before the game: 'I think Chris has done an amazing job. He took the job on in very difficult circumstances and I think, for any manager, unless you're going into an international job and you've got a squad full of world-class players, then to get results immediately is very,

very difficult.' O'Neill went on to pinpoint Coleman's particular strengths: 'Chris, like me, had to get to know the players. Everyone talks about Wales and says they've got Gareth Bale, which is a very big plus, but Chris has done particularly well to have one of the top players of the world in his squad and to have managed that relationship with Real Madrid to have Bale available so regularly and obviously very well integrated into the squad. It's a testament to Chris' man-management skills that he's been able to create such a tight-knit squad. Wales are very, very good. I thought they were good throughout qualifying – they were always in a strong position to get over the line and I'm delighted that they'll be in France too.'

For Northern Ireland, as for Wales – although this was a friendly that had originally been suggested nine months previously, before the Belgium home game – there were particular benefits to the timing of the fixture this time around. O'Neill felt Wales shared particular similarities with his side's Euro 2016 group-stage opponents Poland, should Gareth Bale and Aaron Ramsey start for the Dragons. Unfortunately for O'Neill, they didn't. Wales opted for a more experimental side, featuring some players who had been on the fringes of the squad for the qualifying campaign, as well as others who hadn't been in a Wales squad for some time – not to mention a front three of George Williams, David Cotterill and Sam Vokes that had never played together before.

The result for Wales was a somewhat incoherent performance against an exceptionally well-organised side that was full of confidence, having gone undefeated for over a year. However, it was still an exceptionally valuable exercise for both the manager and the players in whittling down the squad to the final 23-man group that would be selected to go to France. 'It has been a really crazy two years, making my debut for Wales then kicking on with Fulham, playing in qualifying matches for Wales, getting injured, fighting back, getting into the Fulham squad again, going on loan,' the young wing wizard George Williams said of his year to date. He went on to discuss his express intention of proving himself against Northern Ireland: 'I definitely felt I had a point to prove in the Northern Ireland game. I knew that I was never a certainty to get into the final 23 for France – I knew that the opportunity I got to play in March was perfect for me to show what I can do and why I should be going.' The likes of George Williams and Jonny Williams certainly did that on the night, with the latter coming on with Joe Allen and Simon Church, while the former was a thorn in the side of the Northern Irish for an hour before making way for Lloyd Isgrove as a substitute. Wales ground out a 1–1 draw before heading into their next friendly three days later against Ukraine.

Emyr Huws this time took his chance to shine, starting in midfield against a very physical, very aggressive side; but he looked totally at home, linking up with Jonny Williams and Joe Allen for the majority of the game. The trio dominated possession and showed numerous neat touches and flicks, though the Dragons still struggled to create very much going forward – but what do you expect when Bale, Ramsey and Robson-Kanu are out? Wales would go on to concede a soft goal from a rehearsed free-kick routine, where Andriy Yarmolenko capitalised on being the first to react as a Ukrainian free-kick was dinked over the wall to the forward's feet, from which he scored a brilliant half-volley. Chris Coleman's men would never recover that deficit, but it was hardly panic stations as otherwise Wales were defensively pretty solid and spent most of their time in possession on the edge of Ukraine's final third – they just couldn't find a way through.

I remember being on talkSPORT the day after that game, talking about my previous book, *The Dragon Roars Again*. Andy Jacobs and Paul Hawksbee were great guys; really receptive, unbiased and – as you'd expect – they were scarily knowledgeable, even about Wales. Even they, however, asked if Wales could win without Bale and Ramsey. If they were asking that, you can imagine what the naysayers were saying about Wales having won only one of their last six games at the time. However, this only played into Chris Coleman's hands in the long-term as it totally fuelled the underdog mentality. 'I understand why people were worried going into the competition after struggling for results really, and – I don't know if it helps me because I've been a part of this squad, I've been involved and I know the players and their characters – I just feel that we're not a side who perform well in friendlies,' former Wales international Owain Tudur Jones noted in the build-up to the tournament. 'We're always at our best when it's competitive, when there's something on the line – people were saying before the tournament that we'd won one game in the last six, but I just think we're not a world-class side who can turn up on any given day and win friendlies. We're at our best when there's something on it, when there's a little bit of pressure, people are doubting the players – that brings the best out of our performances.'

There would be over two months between those two games and the Sweden encounter in June, where the optimism and realisation of what an incredible summer lay ahead of us all really hit home, but even in that time there were more bumps in the road to contend with. Wales fans have always worried about injuries to their star players, and never more so than on the eve of the fabled Euro 2016 squad announcement in May, where Chris Coleman was scheduled to announce his 29-man provisional squad for a training camp in Portugal ahead of the Euros. It was at this point that there was one hammer blow of an injury for the Welsh to contend with: Joe Ledley broke his leg on 7 May. Coming on as a second-half substitute for Crystal Palace, Joe Ledley's beard didn't grace the Selhurst Park pitch for long as he succumbed to what he initially thought was a calf injury just 11 minutes later and left the field of play.

Finding out the next day that it was a fracture, Ledley naturally thought his season and hopes of reaching the Euros were over. However, here's the man himself telling all about how he made the fastest recovery ever from a fibular fracture: 'I'd get up at five o'clock every morning and catch a train to St. John's Hospital to use the oxygen chamber there for about an hour and a half, then I'd get a train back to the training ground, go swimming, use the bike, altitude training, then get treatment too and get back home at about 5 p.m., 6 p.m. every day. So it was hard work, but I had to make sacrifices and it was worthwhile in the end – I wouldn't change a bit of it.' Ledley also made a point of paying tribute to Crystal Palace and Wales physiotherapist Sean Connelly for overseeing his rehabilitation: 'Sean was instrumental to my recovery. I worked with him at Cardiff too, and he treated me a lot of times there so he knows my body just as well as I do. At first when the scan results came through, we were both gutted, but he believed I could recover. Once he said that, we put in the hard work and soon the strength came back, the bone started to heal – some people said we'd need to pin it, some thought we shouldn't. Then we just had scans every few days, and you could see the bone healing pretty well so we left it, and it was the right decision.' Ledley would make it back into training for the pre-tournament camp, just three weeks after the break – what more can I say? That's just unbelievable, and it provided such a boost to everyone both involved with the team and supporting Wales as fans.

Chris Coleman renewed his contract with Wales the week before the Portugal camp too, providing another boost for everyone concerned as the manager agreed a two-year extension. Then it was out to Portugal to get down to business. Only playing one friendly between the end of the domestic season and the tournament raised a lot of eyebrows – particularly as England opted to go for three preparatory matches for some reason, but they didn't have Ryland Morgans running the show for them on the performance side of things. If the physical preparation of the players isn't right, then naturally the mental side won't be either, but Wales got everything spot on. Ian Mitchell had really looked into Olympic and World Cup preparations, speaking to a number of other performance psychologists who said that it was key for the preparation camp to be as similar as possible to the tournament camp, so everything in Portugal was practically identical to Dinard. The layout of the pitch with a marquee gym next to it, ten minutes away from the hotel – two separate entities for working and relaxing – everything was thought of, in exceptional detail.

'I had a lot of conversations with players in Portugal,

and we also started to build the group and the togetherness out there too, so they were doing a lot of work with me away from the pitch – small challenges, or high-pressure situations,' Ian Mitchell said of the mental preparations he put the players through while out in Portugal for the week. 'We were putting them into small groups of five or six, where they'd have to work out a group challenge of golf-putting tasks under pressure – totally irrelevant to football, but a football theme within them, because they'd develop their decision-making. We'd put distractions in there too, to distract them from the task at hand – visual distractions, noise distractions – then after those challenges they'd have a meeting with me and I'd debrief them on how they could take the key themes from those challenges into the tournament. The main message was that there'd be a lot of distractions in France, and we had to remember what we were going there for, so that message was well embedded within everything we did and the players were very well prepared for what they'd face in the tournament as a result.'

Many since the tournament's conclusion will have seen the players post pictures, videos, messages and memories on social media and they all got their own share of attention from fans, but the one that probably stood out the most was David Cotterill's video of a few of the players performing a Haka in front of the rest of the squad, in their underwear! That was part of the Dragon Court, which started in Portugal – again led by Mitchell – and was carried on throughout the tournament. Any successful team knows that getting your players to perform cohesively together on the pitch is one thing, but if you can get them to enjoy each other's company off it then they'll perform a thousand times better when it counts as a result. That's certainly true of the Wales squad, as we know, but Mitchell detailed exactly what happened in 'court': 'We put the players into teams and challenged them every day – it could be a quiz, or anything like that – whatever it was, there was a daily challenge that I took charge of. Players could get fined on certain aspects – late for meetings, wrong clothes or whatever – then that came to a court on Friday. Normally it's called the Kangaroo Court but we called it the Dragon Court, because we wanted to play on that Welsh identity. I facilitated that every Friday and there was always a massive build-up – everybody was excited for it. Chris was the judge, the coaches were the Grand Jury and then the players would nominate a player for a forfeit – singing, dancing, a phone call home on loudspeaker in front of 50 or 60 people – and if you were successful, you got points for your team etc.' Reading that, you're probably laughing, wondering what the likes of Joe Ledley, James Collins or Wayne Hennessey got up to, but there was a very real purpose for utilising the court in the team's spare time. 'Joking aside, socially it was good fun, but it had an important underpinning, because we had a long time out in France where we weren't playing football and the court took the focus away from the pressure and expectation of football a little bit. It had to be managed very carefully, but Chris told me at the end of the camp that he thought it was a stroke of genius.'

Mitchell was also involved in the most difficult aspect of Portugal – telling the 29 players whether they'd made it into the squad or not. During the weeks and months since qualification, everyone and their dog had had an opinion about who should be in the squad. I remember working on a piece for Golwg360 where four of us picked squads, and they were all pretty much identical except for one player here or there. One player I and many others thought would make it into the 23 was Emyr Huws, but he wasn't selected and the outcry on social media was fairly substantial, especially because even though Joe Ledley trained in Portugal, many were still unsure whether he'd play. 'Emyr Huws not being there was the big shock for me. You could more or less pick the squad weeks in advance – everyone was doing their little blogs and pieces on who's in and who's out – but I was very surprised he wasn't there,' Sgorio's Dylan Ebenezer said of Emyr Huws' omission from the squad. 'In the cold light of day I think he'd have been a better option, but Chris Coleman knew what he was doing. You can understand not taking him because he's so young, but it's cruel, because he has a massive, massive future. I still feel sorry for him – he must have been so gutted watching on from home – but I'm sure we'll see much more from him in the future. As Osian said afterwards, he has the potential to be a future captain, so fingers crossed he fulfils that potential!'

Sweden would be where Wales were expected to continue fulfilling their potential, as Chris Coleman's squad travelled out to Stockholm to take part in their only preparatory friendly. Opting to run with a similar format to that employed a year previously when Wales faced Belgium in Cardiff, the players took part in a friendly match played amongst themselves behind closed doors whilst out in Portugal – worryingly resulting in a knock for Hal Robson-Kanu, adding to concerns about Joe Allen and, despite his miraculous recovery up to that point, Joe Ledley. Sweden would prove to be the last opportunity for Coleman's Dragons to get some minutes under their belts before the tournament started in Bordeaux less than a week later. Welsh fans wouldn't get the chance to wave their players off in style with a final home game at Cardiff before the tournament, or to celebrate a victory which could have spirits and optimism at their most potent within Wales since qualification was secured nine months earlier. No, exactly the opposite in fact – because, out in Stockholm, Wales were comprehensively taken apart by Sweden, and then the questions really started to be asked. Even the most loyal and optimistic of journalists following Wales said Chris Coleman's side would struggle to score a goal in France if they produced similar performances in the tournament to the one in this friendly, as the Dragons lost 3–0 to a Swedish side that barely broke a sweat on the way to victory.

Alarm bells were ringing all of a sudden, and the bubble seemed to have well and truly burst – had Wales peaked too early? Was qualifying a fluke? Had the players been worked too hard in Portugal? Was the pressure getting to everyone? These were all questions being asked by everyone, from Joe Bloggs on the street to Chris Coleman, who was also very downhearted. 'I spoke to Chris about this after the Sweden game and he was a bit downbeat, saying he felt they'd been knocked out of the tournament already and we hadn't even got there yet,' Kit Symons said of the manager's state of mind after losing to Sweden. 'People were also questioning us, saying we hadn't played enough friendlies, but the friendlies didn't mean a thing to me and I said that to Chris. All I was concerned about was getting everyone on the pitch and fit for Slovakia. We knew with everyone fit what shape we would play and what the starting XI would be, so there was nothing to find out from the friendlies. If you look at the friendlies, they caused England more problems than they did anything else, because no-one knew who their best team was, what their best formation was. We knew all of that long before, so Chris used them for other purposes. The friendlies were almost a waste of time for us. We were able to give time to other players, a chance to look at a few players for the squad, but the three friendlies had no bearing on the Slovakia game. A Welsh team without Ramsey and Bale is very different to a Welsh team with them, so what are you going to learn from playing games without them? If those boys hadn't been fit for the tournament then it might have been different, but we knew they would be. Some people questioned if the bubble was burst or whatever, but we haven't got enough bodies or strength in depth to play loads of games and try all these different things, and certainly from England's perspective, doing that caused more problems than anything else.'

The team spent a long time in the dressing room after the game, and the media were waiting a while to speak to them. It was a disheartening performance to say the least, but in the end perhaps it was a good thing to have happened in hindsight, because of the wake-up call it gave the team. Anyway, as Kit Symons noted, the friendlies didn't really matter and Wales' Dragons made their way to France straight after the game to get their preparations for the real action underway in earnest.

Pre-tournament Friendly Results:
November 13th, 2015: Wales 2–3 Netherlands
March 24th, 2016: Wales 1–1 Northern Ireland
March 28th, 2016: Ukraine 1–0 Wales
June 5th, 2016: Sweden 3–0 Wales

CHAPTER 2

Dinard – Wales' *Chez Moi* for the tournament

'It reminded us of Tenby and the Pembrokeshire Coast
– it was very much like that part of the world,
very much a home from home for us.'

MARK EVANS, FAW

LOGISTICS ARE THE last thing any football fan in the world will think about when evaluating the successes or failures of their beloved national side at major tournaments. Tactics, personnel, the run of fixtures, rest days between games, the weather... heck, even the colour of the kit their team wore and other random superstitions will generally be considered as more important contributors to a team's fortunes at a major tournament than the logistics by your average supporter. Logistics are exceptionally important though, and encompass many key issues: where the team trains, where they stay, how they travel, what facilities there are for the players to utilise in their downtime, how quiet the area is... Anything you can think of that the team might have to do is meticulously planned beforehand, and the choice of a team's base for the tournament is a vital decision that can have drastic knock-on effects on performances on the pitch.

Graham Hunter wrote in his book *Spain: The inside story of La Roja's historic treble* about the particular lengths that the Royal Spanish Football Federation (RFEF) went to in order to ensure the perfect team base was prepared for them in the 2008 Euros. The RFEF eventually decided to base the Spanish squad in the remote Stubai valley, because of its close proximity to the location of two of Spain's group games in Innsbruck, Austria. They totally scrapped their original plans to make camp in Solothurn, Switzerland – nearly 400 km away from Innsbruck, and even further away from Salzburg, where Spain's final group game was played. Despite the fact that Spain had David Villa, David Silva, Fernando Torres, Cesc Fàbregas, Carles Puyol, Iker Casillas et al. in that Euro 2008-winning squad, would they have won it if the team had had to travel 2,500 km more than they ended up doing in the group stages? I'm going to say no. Kurt Jara, the former Austrian international and Valencia midfielder, was instrumental in arranging the Spanish squad's stay in the Stubai valley, convincing then-Spain manager Luis Aragonés to base the team there. Aragonés naturally saw the benefits of the location, and his players later said what an inspired choice they thought it was.

Mark Evans, as Head of the FAW's International Department, played a similar role for Wales. He lead a vast team of incredibly dedicated staff from numerous departments within the FAW and the Welsh Football Trust on their vitally important quest to find and develop the best possible location for Wales to base themselves in order to maximise their tournament performance. Mark has been working at the FAW since the days where their offices didn't have enough telephones for their employees to have one each, enjoying 27 years of service at the Association as one of the many employees who literally live their lives to support and ensure the best for Welsh football. After the tournament, his colleague Peter Barnes called Mark the 'unsung hero' of Welsh football, whilst Rob Dowling – another of Mark's many colleagues – had this to say of him: 'Mark is quite simply the Godfather of Welsh Football. He has worked for the FAW for so long and he's revered by everyone... the cheers he'd get when walking around the stadiums at the Euros was incredible. Everyone at UEFA knows and has a massive respect for him, and his beard is just quite incredible really. The amount of work he does is immense – he never stops and he's been absolutely unbelievable for the Football Association of Wales.'

In the end, a small town called Dinard in Brittany – a region that has strong cultural ties to Wales with over 40 towns twinned with Welsh ones, as well as numerous other social links – played host to the Wales squad for five weeks as they embarked on their Euro 2016 odyssey. Mark was happy to speak to me about the process of selecting Dinard, outlining just why it was the perfect setting for Wales to work from as they chased glory in France that summer.

Jamie Thomas: How soon did the process of looking for a training base begin, and can you talk us through a brief overview of the kind of work you did to narrow your choice down to Dinard?

Mark Evans: After we beat Belgium, to be honest with you we all sort of realised then that something special was happening. We had a phone call from UEFA – specifically from a gentleman called Lars Hemkes, UEFA's Team Services Manager – who basically said we were top of the group, we looked like we were going to make it and that we'd need to go and talk to them, because we needed to start looking at bases. Dai Griffiths (Wales Team Equipment Manager) and I went over to UEFA to talk to them about how the system and the process worked. We already had a brochure of the 61 Team Bases available to choose from in France, and we'd looked through it, but we asked how soon we'd have to decide and UEFA told us to start the process there and then. Over the course of that summer, Amanda Smith (Wales Team Operations Manager) went over to France with Osian Roberts and Chris Coleman and had a look at facilities down in the south of France first – I remember we chose a base in Perpignan initially as a starting point – and Amanda also went north on the same trip, where we reserved a hotel in Croissy-sur-Seine.

Then we started having conversations with people who had been to France before for similar events. One of the people we spoke to was Adrian Bevington (former Managing Director at the Football Association), who mentioned the north and places like Dinard. We also spoke to the Local Organising Committee in Paris, with a gentleman called Andreas Phillips who was magnificent, and he gave us five or six places to send Chris Coleman and Osian Roberts over to visit on his recommendation and just see what they think... and the story is very true, that when Chris and Osian walked into the hotel in Dinard, they rang me a few minutes later and said 'This is the one!' That was that really, but they'd gone there on their own so myself, my staff and Amanda went out there a few weeks later with Dai Griffiths to do our checks. We agreed with them, and the basics were all sorted very quickly. It could have been a very long, drawn-out process – because even when we went to the draw, for example, some people were still looking for bases – but we were always happy with what we had. But then the planning started with how we wanted to do it, regarding the training pitches, the media centre and the gym facilities. Two days after the Andorra game, once we'd all got over our hangovers from celebrating, we flew all of the staff out to Dinard for last-minute checks on a one-day visit, so we knew everything we'd have to sort out in the months ahead. It was a very intensive day, but very useful.

JT: What specifically about Dinard made you all so sure that this was the right place to base yourselves?

ME: Dinard had one thing we really wanted, because it was in Brittany and we always said we wanted somewhere with cultural links – that was a big thing for us. So when Chris and Osian said Dinard was the place, that was perfect. We didn't want an exclusive hotel either: we wanted to be mixing with people, because we did a lot of fact-finding, speaking to people like Thierry Henry, Adrian Bevington and others, and gathered a lot of information. I spoke to the Dutch as well, when they came over for the friendly in November, and what they said was that having an exclusive hotel was great, but in the end you can get cabin fever, because you're the only ones there. Having said that, we wanted the place to be quiet or away from the town, which the hotel in Dinard was, so that was great.

The main thing though was this: Chris Coleman's main proviso is that the training pitches are up to scratch. He isn't too fussy about the hotel, although it obviously has to be a good one – and he liked the training pitches in Dinard. They needed work, obviously, but he was very impressed. He liked everything about the area: the geography, the way it looked, how the pitches were enclosed with a dressing room block, and obviously we all loved the fact that the people of Dinard were so receptive to us. Whatever we asked them to do, they did it, and that was true until the very end. Chris loved the hotel but he liked the training ground even more, and the combination of the two won it for us. It was quiet: a small town, out of the way, and we practically had the airport to ourselves so whenever we had to travel we left the hotel at 12:45 and we were in the air at 1:30. Everything about Dinard just made it the perfect team base for us really. You just couldn't fault it at all, it was fantastic!

JT: How do you go about securing a place like that? Were there any complications with the hotel or the facilities at all?
ME: UEFA contract these hotels to act as team bases during the tournament, so we knew how much it would cost us because it was there in the brochure. These places aren't cheap, but we looked at a place in Paris that was twice the price of Dinard, so we knew what we were getting and we were happy with the price and so on. The interesting thing was that we weren't the first team to pick that hotel – the first team to pick it was Portugal, then they decided they wanted to be closer to Paris so they changed their minds... which is a bit funny, considering how our paths ended up crossing.

Securing the hotel was fairly straightforward, compared to the rest of the logistics. The real challenges were the training ground, the media centre, the gym – those things took a lot of effort and time to organise and perfect. We brought a lot of attention to the area and we were very keen to celebrate our links with them, so we had the Breton flag flying outside the team hotel in Cardiff before we left for France. We took the Breton flag with us everywhere we went, as well as the Welsh flag. The only issue Dinard had was that we didn't want to announce it too quickly, because we wanted everything prepared and perfect before we unveiled it to everyone. It was always an open secret, but we wanted to make sure the pitch was right and so on, because we were mindful of some of the press other teams had had previously when pitches weren't quite ready. But the people of Dinard were magnificent and everything was perfect for us, to be honest with you!

JT: I've seen pictures of the hotel – it looked really beautiful and they went to town to make the squad welcome. Describe the location to us, if you can.
ME: The hotel was on the headland overlooking the town, with a magnificent view over the bay. If you ever get a chance to go there, you should! It reminded us of Tenby and the Pembrokeshire Coast – it was very much like that part of the world, very much a home from home for us. It was very out of the way. It was a spa hotel, more or less geared towards the middle-aged clientele, so most of the people didn't have a clue who Gareth Bale was, to be perfectly honest with you! We were able to wander around, do what we wanted. We had Tai Chi classes in the evening and nobody would bother us or come over or anything like that. You could walk into the town and have an ice cream; the boys went down and played football on the beach with the kids; nobody bothered us at all – if they did, it was in the right way, but we were never swamped with crowds of people or anything like that. Every shop window had a Euro 2016 display, and many of them had Welsh things as well. The chocolatiers there were absolutely amazing as well, with one of them making a big Wales flag out of chocolate – you can't not be impressed with that!

JT: How much work did the training facilities and the media centre take? Some of the journalists I've spoken to have said that Wales' media centre was the best of them all.

ME: I'd go with that, but Kevin Moon (Welsh Football Trust Facilities Manager) was the man responsible for putting all of that together. There was a college next to the training centre, so we basically took over the main assembly hall and turned it into our media centre. I have to say, once again, that the Mayor of Dinard was fantastic in clearing the whole booking for us. What we've also got is the best branding image in UEFA, the '#TogetherStronger' branding, and we were just able to integrate that straight into the media centre and kit it out, because we were determined to make sure that the media had a great time.

The only thing we had to deliver that was out of our hands a little bit was the training pitches. We didn't do much to the pitches actually: we just reseeded it, cut it and so on, and by the end it was magnificent. The biggest thing we did there in terms of change was the gym. We installed a marquee gym there – Ryland Morgans, our Head of Performance, had a vision of using it as a one-stop shop and that's exactly what we did, and it worked so well. The players went down at 10 a.m. every morning, did their pre-session activation, completed their training session, then did a bit more work in the gym, had a shower and went back to the hotel to relax. It was important to have it that way, because there was that key difference between locations. In the morning they left the hotel and went to work between 10 a.m. and 1.30 p.m., doing training, tactical work, anything like that, then afterwards they went straight back to the hotel, which was the relaxing area in every sense. They could get treatment, they could go to the masseurs, the physios; or they could play table tennis, they could watch TV, play their PlayStations together or whatever they wanted to do!

JT: Did the players have any requests with regards to what they wanted the hotel to include, at all? I heard one thing in particular you gave them had a special effect...
ME: The one thing with the players – we've been doing this for a long time with them now and dealing with any requests they might have – but the one thing we have to have in every single hotel is this: table tennis. They love table tennis! Some of them should turn pro one day, they're that good. The environment – whether it's table tennis, darts, the PlayStations, whatever – we've always done that, but we wanted to take it a bit further this time, because they're all on social media, they're all on Twitter, so we wanted to bring that into the hotel for them. In the breakout area in the players' corridor, on the wall there was a big interactive screen that they could go and touch and look at and see what was happening at home via social media. That was a luxury at the start, they didn't really use it; but as we progressed through the group it became really important because of the bubble we were in, and we didn't know what was going on at home sometimes. When we were getting the tweets from the schools of their pupils singing the anthem or the Joe Ledley song and sending it to us, then it brings you home and made us realise that something was happening back in Wales. The players didn't really go near it to start

43

with, but as it went on everyone wanted to see what was going on back home and the impact we were having.

JT: Then, after doing all of that hard work to make sure everything was ready for when you arrived as a group for the first time, how did everyone react and were any of the players particularly taken by it?
ME: It was a bit strange getting there after the Sweden game. We left Stockholm straight after the game, but landed in France at about 10.45 p.m. Every team that went to France got a welcome from the Mayor of the town they were staying in with a red carpet and all the trimmings and everything, but of course we landed quite late at night so it was a bit surreal, and it was dark, so when we got to the hotel most people were quite tired and just went to bed. In a way, it was the next morning when everyone started to appreciate the location and the beauty of where we were. I don't think they got the full effect until then, but the rooms were totally unique, as they were all personalised with photos and messages for each individual player on their bedroom walls, so they got that when they arrived, but they didn't get the full effect until the next morning.

All the players were out on the decking in the morning having their coffees, just trying to take everything in at that point, because that first day was a rest day. I think that setting was perfect for them, especially the way it was all split up as I mentioned earlier. Then when we came back to Dinard after the games it was almost like a haven, where everyone was looking after us and the welcomes back were getting louder and louder. We were left alone in the hotel, nobody bothered us, and we accounted for two thirds of the hotel. Some people might have thought they weren't interested, but they really were. When we came back and all of the air-horns were going off, the harps were playing and we were all being applauded on the way back into the hotel, it was massive for the players to come back to that and then they were boosted as they went back into their routine and prepared for the next match.

The players were all taken by it. A lot of the boys played golf out there, but some of the boys used to go into town every day, or fairly often, to get a coffee or just chill out. They didn't take any security with them, they didn't have to – we just had to know where they were for the doping controls – but they all just appreciated the fact that it was so relaxed, that they could walk into Dinard, people would say hello to them, but otherwise they were left alone. I think they enjoyed being there because they were accepted for being there and having a job to do. Dinard was proud to see them there, but other than that they let us get on with our jobs.

The point of this chapter was just to give a tiny insight into the incredible amount of work the FAW put into organising everything that goes on around the team. A lot of people assume that these teams just turn up at tournaments and are ready to go and play to try and win the thing, but it just doesn't work like that! Our achievement was beyond our wildest dreams before the tournament began, and there is no doubt in my mind that we would never have found ourselves as far on in the tournament as we did had it not been for Dinard and the meticulous planning that went into Wales' set-up away from the pitch. There is so much more behind the scenes to think about, as Mark's answers go some way towards demonstrating.

The likes of Mark Evans, Amanda Smith, Dai Griffiths, Ian Gwyn Hughes (FAW Head of Public Affairs), Peter Barnes, Rob Dowling, Lauren Jones (FAW Media Executive), Gwyn Derfel (WPL Secretary), Kevin Moon and so many more work their backsides off day and night to make sure that everything is absolutely perfect for our Dragons before they take to the pitch and bring immense pride to our fantastic nation – the team behind the team, as they call it. They're just exceptional, every single one of them, and they deserve at least as much thanks for fulfilling our dreams (and then some!) as the players who have taken to the pitch over the last 18 months. Bravo, Mesdames et Messieurs, bravo! Now on to Bordeaux, where everything suddenly started to get very real!

CHAPTER 3

Wales vs Slovakia

Nouveau Stade de Bordeaux – 11 June 2016

'I think Ben has watched that block quite a few
times since to be fair, so he doesn't need to be
told it was an amazing block – he knows!'

JONNY WILLIAMS, WALES INTERNATIONAL

WE SHOULD HAVE known from the venues. It sounds
strange to say, but the architecture, the vibrancy
and simplistic beauty of the stadiums where Wales
contested their historic fixtures at Euro 2016 – each of
them having a unique characteristic perfectly suited
to the momentous events that were witnessed within
them – should have told the Red Wall that it was in for
an incredible few weeks on the continent! How fitting
that in Nouveau Stade de Bordeaux – the stunning
modernist arena chosen for Wales' opening gambit
at the European Championship against the Marek
Hamšík-inspired Slovakia – there would be nowhere
to hide from the action, as if anyone in there would
have wanted to. Even when wandering around the
concourse prior to the game or at half-time – whether

that be socialising, queuing to collect your pint of 0.5% alcohol lager, or simply looking for the loo – beyond the sea of red shirts meandering with you, you could still see the pitch clear as day. At every turn, it was still completely visible, the concourse acting as the perfect viewing gallery sandwiched between two tiers of thunderous noise. It was as if the stadium itself was begging its occupants: 'Please, watch that pitch – something special is going to happen on there today.'

Personally, my Euro 2016 journey had started with a cancelled overnight train from Paris to Bordeaux that left my mates and me playing football with some Spaniards under the Eiffel Tower through the night, but walking up the steps of my block in the stadium in Bordeaux, I stopped dead at the top when I could see the arena in its entirety and pretty much broke down. It can't have been more than a dozen paces from the concourse at that point, but in some ways it felt like climbing Everest, with every step getting so much easier as my friends and I inched ever closer to a sight we'd all been waiting a lifetime to see. A group of French lads were trotting up the stairs in front of us, decked out in Wales tops and chanting 'ALLEZ LES ROUGES! ALLEZ LES ROUGES! ALLEZ LES ROUGES!' Not only had Chris Coleman's men touched the Welsh nation, it seemed, but even the French were behind us. Many more joined Wales' list of admirers as the tournament went on, thanks to the excellence of the players on the pitch and, in no small part, to the relentless support and chanting from the fans, who kept stadiums rocking and cities awake at night with their passion and excitement for the stage they were all given to perform on. This moment at the top of the stairs in Bordeaux, the buzz in the city, getting there, living there, everything about the country and what followed in Euro 2016 for Wales felt so right. What we all saw on that afternoon in the south of France was sheer perfection: an ocean of red, the stands rammed with the most dedicated of our Dragons' disciples, each and every one of us wiping tears from our eyes. Serbia, Russia, Romania, Scotland (twice), Yugoslavia – all of it washed away by waves of relief and ecstasy as our minds reeled with exhilaration at the prospect of the fortnight ahead of us, never mind what came afterwards. What we all saw in front of us that day was penance from the footballing gods for all of the times they'd sinned against our nation over the years, and it was magnificent.

As *Hen Wlad Fy Nhadau* bellowed around the stadium, France itself surely ground to a standstill. Gary Speed – undoubtedly watching over the events unfolding from up there in the sky – surely heard every word of it clear as day, singing along with us. It was absolutely deafening; Wales' way of announcing their arrival at the summer's tournament, with the incredible level of noise letting everyone know we were there to stay! Raymond Verheijen was also very

49

moved by the unbelievable atmosphere created by the Welsh supporters during the Slovakia match, and throughout the tournament, as he noted that the fans were among the star attractions that the tournament had to offer. 'Even when you're just watching the games on television, you can hear those Welsh fans constantly. The typical Welsh songs, the anthem, the fans were singing non-stop – you could hear the Gary Speed songs loud and clear in every game, and that really gave me goosebumps. I think that the main attraction of Euro 2016 was the fans – the Welsh, the Irish, the Northern Irish, the Icelandic fans – they gave an extra dimension to this tournament, and made for good entertainment in every game.'

On this gloriously sunny, humid afternoon in Bordeaux, there wasn't a dry eye in sight as the anthems came to an end and Wales were within seconds of kicking off a tournament that we'd all waited a lifetime for, despite most of us having come to believe that this moment would never arrive. Dylan Ebenezer summarised the mood in the beautiful city of Bordeaux perfectly: 'It was everything we've ever dreamed of! It was one of those moments where you realise that despite what you've been dreaming of, it's not often that the actual reality of it is a thousand times better, but that's exactly what happened ahead of the Slovakia game! It was just staggering: the whole build-up, getting to Bordeaux and just seeing the Welsh shirts pour in over the course of a few days was something I'll never ever forget. It was just a massive, joyous celebration at that point though – people didn't care! It's funny now, looking back, that we're all moaning and saying we could have won the tournament, but in Bordeaux there was none of that as everyone was just ecstatic to be there and be a part of history. Wales had qualified, in a beautiful city, with a wonderful stadium, but the atmosphere in Bordeaux the night before the game will stay with me forever – just one big party, everyone singing, dancing and hugging each other just to celebrate the fact that we'd made it to that point.'

What tells you above all else that this was an incredibly emotional, moving occasion, though, was the reaction of the players when they lined up to sing the anthems. We commonly think of footballers as these absolute machines who think only about winning and celebrating success. They generally don't get taken by any atmosphere or buzz inside the stadium, just focus fully on the task at hand and overcoming the challenge put in front of them. Wales' fans, though, are so incredible that every single one of the players I spoke to about the tournament told me how emotional they became when the anthems were being sung. Our inspirational leader, Ashley Williams, admitted to being emotional on four occasions in that first game against Slovakia, such was the intensity of the occasion. In truth, it's totally understandable that the players would be affected in such a way. I mean, if you were wearing a red shirt in Bordeaux, you were probably crying (or 'rubbing dust out of your eye') at some point during the day, but the players in particular experienced totally new phenomena in this game, away from the pitch as well as on it.

When the team get together for a game in Cardiff, they're generally based a few miles outside the city, well away from the buzz that is building, until they travel into the city on the coach on the day of the game. This game was totally different, though, as the FAW's Rob Dowling pointed out. 'I remember going to a meeting in the hotel on the morning of the game. There were a lot of fans staying nearby and the windows in the hotel were open, so all we could hear constantly throughout that meeting and the day was the fans singing. All of the players would have heard it; we all heard it – there was just this buzz and excitement inside and outside the hotel. All of a sudden it felt like we were at the Euros, with the fans all congregated around our hotel and the players were mobbed by them as they went for their walk in the morning – I don't think I've ever known emotion like I experienced that day in Bordeaux. To see all of the fans constantly crying on screens, we were all affected by that and the anthems in particular. There were hundreds and hundreds of fans outside the hotel, everyone clapping us, stopping our cars... just a very emotional, unforgettable experience.'

On top of that, before the game the players were all shown video messages from their families and friends, wishing them all the best ahead of what was sure to be an incredibly glorious occasion, regardless of the result. Naturally all of the players were touched by that, contributing even further to the incredible emotional level of this unforgettable occasion. Chris Coleman was on top form too, revelling in the moment, with Mark Evans recalling a brief conversation with the Welsh manager moments before kick-off. 'The moment that I got really emotionally filled up was in Bordeaux: once during the anthem, and once when Chris Coleman spoke to me after the anthem. When Ashley Williams swaps the match pennant with the opposition captain, I go and collect it from him to look after, and as I turn around and go back, I always shake Chris Coleman's hand to say good luck. But this time as I did so, he just said "Enjoy it!" I just filled up there and then – what a perfect thing to say to someone like myself. Not good luck, just enjoy it. That Bordeaux experience, before we'd even kicked a ball, that was it – it was just perfect. Then it just got better!'

The resolve of the Welsh nation, however, was tested almost instantly. Hamšík danced his way through Chris Coleman's defence, finding himself one-on-one with Liverpool's Danny Ward – a late inclusion after Wayne Hennessey had suffered back spasms in the team hotel the night before – and dinked the ball over the goalkeeper's 6' 3" frame. One supporter perfectly summarised the emotions of the entire nation in that moment, when Hamšík's effort appeared to be flying into an empty net: 'Within a handful of touches from that little fella (Hamšík), he'd sliced our defence open, found himself with just Ward to beat and lobbed him to score what looked like a certain goal. In three minutes our campaign slogan seemed to go from '#TogetherStronger' to 'Here we go again' – but then Big Ben swung in and saved the day!' Quite possibly Wales' tournament too! Ben Davies should have been included in UEFA's team of the tournament because of that clearance alone, never mind his impressive composure on the ball and his tremendous ability to read the game, which helped Wales at both the attacking and defensive ends of the pitch in every game Davies played.

I'll never forget that sound for as long as I live: the gasping that seemed to get louder as Hamšík's effort inched closer and closer, spinning through the air towards the goal line, and the volume further increasing as the Red Wall realised Davies was sliding in acrobatically to try and save the ball from flying in and sinking Welsh hearts. In one of those incredible twists of fate that really makes you believe that today is going to be your day, Davies did clear the ball. Wales could start again, with their fans doing the seemingly impossible by chanting even louder than before – thanks in no small part to the realisation that they'd almost witnessed their dreams of succeeding in France that summer snatched from before their very eyes. Hamšík had caught the Welsh defence totally off guard. They'd been briefed pre-match that the Slovak – as anyone who watches Hamšík fairly regularly will know – although seriously skilful and always capable of dribbling through defences (as he did against every team he faced in this tournament), likes to shoot early to catch defences by surprise. As a result, his decision to do the opposite this time caught the Welsh defence out, and meant he was able to get as close to scoring as he did. Davies' block was exceptional and – as Jonny Williams would later quip: 'I think Ben has watched that block quite a few times since to be fair, so he doesn't need to be told it was an amazing block – he knows!'

A surprise inclusion in the starting line-up in Bordeaux, Joniesta's first game for Wales – way back when he represented the under-15s – had also been against Slovakia, with Wales losing 5–0. Thankfully, history wouldn't repeat itself on this occasion, but the gutsy attacking midfielder noted the wider significance of Davies' block and how it would go on to have much further-reaching ramifications for Wales' success at Euro 2016: 'If we go 1–0 down there, it's an uphill battle immediately and you never know how those things pan out. Ben's block early on in that game, that set us up for the tournament really – we just had immense belief from that point onwards that something special was going to happen.' It was a perfect barometer of what Wales are all about. Davies' block showed fierce desire and just how willing he was to put everything on the line for his teammates – he could quite easily have done himself some damage chasing that ball. Most players would have left it to go in, such was the apparent hopelessness of the situation at that moment, but Davies' incredible determination proved everyone wrong and showed the continent, who would watch this game back afterwards, exactly what kind of team Wales are, as he cleared the ball and the Dragons were given another chance.

Jonny Williams' inclusion in this game was an inspired choice – one of the many that Chris Coleman made throughout the tournament in terms of his line-up tweaks and the timing of his substitutions. Hal Robson-Kanu took a seat on the bench for this game, as he had lacked match practice in the build-up to the tournament, but the little whippet Joniesta was perfect as his replacement. A persistent menace, hounding opposition defenders and generally making a right nuisance of himself to cause Slovakia all kinds of problems, he slotted seamlessly into the front three with Ramsey and Bale. The trio would rotate positions constantly throughout the game to keep Slovakia guessing, and their relentless energy really limited Slovakia's main threat: their incredible ability to hurt teams in transition. Whenever Wales lost the ball, BANG: those three were there, ready to press the centre backs and the number 6 whilst Wales' wing backs and holding midfielders kept Slovakia's full backs and other midfielders busy. Although there must have been nerves within the Wales camp ahead of this, a game they'd all waited their whole lives to contest, it translated into purpose and joie de vivre as Wales' aggressive pressing game left Slovakia resorting to a long-ball approach that found their forwards hopelessly mismatched against the physicality of Ashley Williams, James Chester and Ben Davies in the Welsh rearguard.

Two more mind-blowing twists of fate were still to come, however, with the first arriving after ten minutes of play. When the oft-labelled Prince of Wales, Gareth Bale, scored his first goal for the Dragons back in 2006, he netted a 25-yard free kick against Slovakia. Ten years later, who was it that scored Wales' first goal at a European Championship, with Wales' first shot on target, from a 25-yard free kick against Slovakia? Yep, that man Gareth Bale! Joniesta was again at the centre of proceedings, winning the free kick for Bale to convert, but what an absolute racket the Wales fans made when that goal was scored! The keeper really should have saved it – he more or less dived out of the way, to be honest, but absolutely nobody in red cared! We were all just immensely happy to be there, whether our Dragons won, lost or drew; but now, after Davies' block and Bale's free-kick, well, we celebrated and sang and leapt around like Wales had just been confirmed as winners of the tournament. The rest of the first half is somewhat of a blur, to be honest with you – none of us could hear ourselves think, and we were all dizzy and exhausted from the constant jumping around and dancing. Gary Speed, Coleman, Bale, Joe Ledley, Hal Robson-Kanu – they all got their turn having their names chanted by the fans. The singing just went on, and on, and on, right up until half-time, where Wales found themselves 1–0 up, having dominated the majority of the first 45 minutes.

Half-time went by in an instant, with everyone in the concourse catching flies as they walked around open-mouthed, contemplating what they'd just witnessed and been a part of. But this is Wales we're talking about... and the second half didn't start as rosily as the first. A change of tactics, formation and personnel for the Slovaks – who had beaten the mighty Spain in qualification and Germany in a pre-tournament friendly, don't forget – suddenly had Wales hanging on to their lead for dear life. Ondrej Duda scored after an hour for the away side, to level the scores at 1–1, but some fantastic, brave decision-making from Coleman turned the game on its head and gave the Dragons the initiative, as Andrew Gwilym – a vastly experienced sports reporter for Westgate Sports Agency – remarked: 'You would have to say that Chris Coleman at this tournament was a man totally sure of his own mind, with total belief in what he and his staff were doing. That's not to say he didn't have that during qualifying, but when he came into the job he didn't have that degree of authority or comfort in the role, and it's something that has had to come gradually over time. Against Slovakia we were at 1–1, we'd not played in a major finals for 60 years... most people at that point, including myself, would have taken the draw. After 75 minutes I'd have taken 1–1, and Chris Coleman could have – maybe the Coleman of a few years ago would have – but he didn't. He looked at it and thought there was still something there for the team, and he was brave enough to go and take it. The two changes he made – bringing Hal Robson-Kanu and Joe Ledley on – were very brave because if Wales had conceded a goal, he'd probably have come under fire. But he had the feel of the game spot on, so it allowed Wales to find the space to play in and go on to win the game – it was a feature of the entire campaign that he made great decisions like that.'

A great decision indeed, as Robson-Kanu came on and was fed by Aaron Ramsey after six minutes on the pitch, mishitting a strike through the legs of Ján Ďurica and into the back of the net. Peeling away from the box, with the rest of Wales' Dragons in tow, HRK's goal was celebrated with a pile-on by the corner flag in front of a set of supporters that were erupting with excitement at the prospect of seeing their beloved little nation succeed on a major international stage and become the first British country ever to win their opening game at a European Championship. The scenes in the crowd were incredible, tear-jerking – absolutely insane, there is no other way to describe it – and this was only the first game!

Whilst everyone rightly lauds the introduction of Robson-Kanu, the arrival of Joe Ledley – yes, the same Joe Ledley who had broken his leg only 35 days prior to all this – onto this incredible stage was a fantastic choice as well. Gaps were suddenly being plugged everywhere, counter-attacks were starting much more quickly, the ball fizzed around much more when Wales had it. This was a guy who had been in tears just over a month earlier at the prospect of missing what he may have thought, with the likes of Emyr Huws coming through the ranks, would be his last chance to be a regular starter for Wales in a major tournament. Yet here he was, running around like a blue-arsed fly to win the initiative back for Wales.

It was particularly touching to see him sharing an emotional embrace with Wales' Head Physio Sean Connelly – who also works for Ledley's club Crystal Palace and oversaw Ledley's rehabilitation from start to finish – just before coming on in the Slovakia match. Wales' bearded hero recalled the experience of succeeding in making it onto the bench in Bordeaux after an incredibly fast recovery: 'I'd never thought before the tournament that I'd make the first game – we'd always aimed for the third – so to come on in the first game and be a part of the goal, and to start every game after that, was a remarkable achievement for everyone involved. I'd played nearly every game in the qualifiers so I obviously wanted to start, but you have to be realistic and I was nowhere near ready to do that. When the national anthem went out I was obviously gutted not to be starting, but I had a lump in my throat because the fans just took over that day, they were absolutely incredible. Then the gaffer told me to warm up, and suddenly I was coming on with the scores at 1–1. Obviously I had to appreciate Sean, you know after everything he did for me. We worked hard together every day for four weeks – he took time out of his own schedule as well. It means so much to me and I'll never forget that – that's why I had to give him a hug before I came on!'

John Martin, a comedian and very close friend of the Speed family, spoke glowingly of Wales' performances in the tournament on the whole, as well as about what happened immediately after scoring the winner against Slovakia, where a flag with Gary Speed's face on it was perfectly placed in the background of the celebrations: 'Gary worked day and night to see the potential of these players realised and have them contesting a major tournament. It was something he tried so hard to achieve as a player himself and something he wanted to achieve as a manager, which is why he started the process of maybe being more professional and thorough than it had been previously. Chris Coleman got these boys to

France in emphatic fashion through qualifying, and you just know Gary was looking down on Chris and these players, cheering and smiling. Seeing his face on a flag in the background as Wales celebrated the winning goal was perfect. Purely coincidence I know, but it was almost as if he was watching over them! These were great times in Welsh football – with many more to come surely – and it is fantastic to see the memory of that great man is still being celebrated today, hand in hand with Chris Coleman's and Wales' incredible successes!'

The reaction from Wales supporters after the match was such that many were convinced Slovakia weren't supposed to be that great an outfit and were surprised at how well they'd performed against Wales at times in the match. That was an incredibly unfair assessment. The fact that they were unbeaten in their last eight games running up to this opening Euro 2016 fixture against the Dragons – a run which included victories over Iceland, Switzerland and the World Champions Germany (who Slovakia beat comfortably) – should have made it abundantly clear to everyone that this was not a team to be trifled with. Even so, some fans were still surprised at Hamšík's quality, the ability of Vladimír Weiss to create havoc every now and then, and the overall performance of Slovakia, although Wales' tactics prevented Ján Kozák's men from performing anywhere near their best.

UEFA's Welsh Football Correspondent Mark Pitman

– usually impervious to emotion in his coverage or analysis of a match – waxed somewhat lyrical about the atmosphere inside the stadium in Bordeaux, as well as Wales' performance on the day. 'There was something unique about the atmosphere: this was THE game, the game that so many had waited for, for so long. I tried to put my finger on what was unique, and I believe it was a collective determination from the fans that this day would not be another day of Welsh football disappointment. Welsh football has had so many over the years, but there seemed to be a feeling that this could not possibly be another one. The fans had so much passion and energy for the anthem, it was hair-raising. You could sense it in the streets before the match, in the stadium – the players could sense it. There were some fine margins that decided the game, but it was beautiful and incredible, and it was a result that really set the tone for the remainder of Wales' campaign.'

Stifling Slovakia's counter-attacking game with aggressive pressing, smart line-up choices and shrewd substitutions – features that would serve Wales well throughout the tournament – Chris Coleman's side had got the job done in an opening game against very strong opposition, where nerves and that sense of anticipation, from both the fans and the players, would be at their highest levels for Wales. Sam Vokes, who didn't feature in Wales' first two games of Euro 2016, but would have a profound impact for the

Dragons later, summed up the experience perfectly: 'What a great day! You could feel the energy and the anticipation before we'd even got to the ground, and I think the way we performed really set us up for the tournament. If we'd lost or drawn that game, we'd have been up against it, so the win was absolutely massive for us because it calmed the nerves and got us off and running. We wanted to get out of the group, and winning the first game was massive in helping us ensure that. Even just warming up, the fans were all there early to sing and cheer and take everything in, and they just made the whole experience even better for us as players, right throughout the tournament. Just a big sea of red... It's a credit to the fans how good they were all tournament, but that Slovakia game was like a big celebration for them – it was really special.'

Ben Davies, the real match-winner in the eyes of many after his third-minute block, admitted when speaking to me after the tournament that he had watched the moment back many a time, but the other special moment for him in the match involved Danny Ward and Jonny Williams. 'Of course I've seen it back! But I've watched Hal's winning goal more times! As a defender it's your job to stop goals, and that's all that I saw that I was doing in that game. The anthem in that game was special, probably the best anthem I've heard Welsh fans sing. I'll always remember this game so well, with it being our first game in a major competition for so long. The nerves, the excitement, it all felt extra special given it was our first game, and to get the win was a very special feeling. Having my good friend Danny Ward come in on such short notice and put in the performance that he did is a great credit to him and to all of the boys in our squad – sharing that moment with two people (Danny and Jonny) who have been teammates of mine since the Under-16's was even better!'

The Welsh fans hadn't given Bordeaux chance to get much sleep the night before the game, as a sea of red on the city's quayside belted out the anthem non-stop, so loud that you couldn't even hear the locals celebrating an opening victory for the Euro 2016 hosts against Romania, and so touching that it garnered attention from all of the country's media the next day (the first of many occasions). It only got better after this victory against Slovakia. My friends and I ended up walking back from the stadium to the city centre, which took about two hours, but when we got back everyone was still singing, hugging, dancing – just really loving and lapping up every single second of the amazing occasion that we were all a part of. Sure, the screens in every pub showing that England had just drawn 1–1 with Russia made for extra pretty viewing, but despite the deafening chants of 'WE! ARE! TOP OF THE LEAGUE! I SAY WE ARE TOP OF THE LEAGUE!' everyone was just so delighted to be there, and the Slovaks were fantastic too, hugging and congratulating us all.

In the main square, I bumped into two fantastic people – Lauren and Holly – who were working on a 'Fans' Reaction' piece for FAW TV and I just had to go over and hug them, because look at what we were standing in the middle of! Probably one of the most beautiful cities in the world, red-shirted fans thronging the streets and *Calon Lân*, *Hen Wlad Fy Nhadau*, the Hal Robson-Kanu chant and countless other amazing sounds all mashed up into what I imagine music must be like in heaven – absolutely breathtaking! I just didn't think it could get any better than that. I was convinced from the minute I left Bordeaux that nothing would top that experience, but it did – it just kept getting better and better and better! In a region best known for its wines, Wales had become the most famous and popular red in the land by far by the time the fans, players and staff reunited again in Lens five days later for an all-British clash against their arch-rivals, Roy Hodgson's England.

Standings after Matchday 1

Pos.	Team	GP	W	D	L	F	A	GD	Pts.
1	Wales	1	1	0	0	2	1	1	3
2	England	1	0	1	0	1	1	0	1
3	Russia	1	0	1	0	1	1	0	1
4	Slovakia	1	0	0	1	1	2	-1	0

Results

Wales 2–1 Slovakia
England 1–1 Russia

CHAPTER 4

England vs Wales

Stade Felix-Bollaert, Lens – 16 June 2016

'We play for the shirt and dragon. I think it's a
jersey that brings something else out of me –
it gives you a feeling as though you're ten foot tall.'

GARETH BALE, WALES INTERNATIONAL

GARETH BALE HAS always appeared to be more of a silent leader than anything else. Quite happy to let other people do the talking for or about him and his immense talents, Bale concentrates on going about his business on the pitch, letting his feet communicate what an instrumental part he plays in the success of what has become a team of unrivalled spirit and passion for the cause. You can't go through a Wales press conference without a question about him, and it's very rare that anyone other than the BBC or Sky gets to put a question to him... but that changed dramatically in France. It became a running joke by the end – 'Welcome to Gareth Bale's weekly press conference,' FAW Head of Communications Ian Gwyn Hughes would say. Not content with simply helping to win matches for Wales on the pitch, Bale decided to follow the lead of his teammates who had shouldered the media responsibilities throughout the qualifying campaign and address the media from the top table, or the stage as it was in the Dinard media centre, in an attempt to win some matches off the pitch. That's not to say that the Wales players or their manager take part in mind games – far from it, in fact, with Chris Coleman repeatedly saying in the past that he'd rather do his talking on the pitch, much like his players – but that Wales' substance and their genuine nature, presenting themselves to the world's press as a bunch of lads who were just there to do their country proud and have fun playing football, disarmed a few people and made them let their guard down, making Wales' job on the pitch that much easier.

Wales were certainly accused of playing mind games, by the English press no less, after Bale made the following comments ahead of the Dragons' opening game against Slovakia. 'If you're Welsh, we feel more pride and passion than anyone else. It's just one of those things. Maybe it's something to do with the small country thing, I don't know – it's just what we're like. I remember when I was young being in a pub with my parents, everyone watching rugby or football. Everyone was together, singing. It's the way we are brought up. I think it probably means a bit more to us because you look at the players we've had that never got this chance. Every team, every time, they all wanted to qualify. For me it (England vs Wales) is probably the standout game of the group stages, but there's no pressure on us. They big themselves up before they've done anything so we're going to go there and we believe we can beat them. They will believe they can beat us but it's one we're relishing. It's like any derby – you never want to lose to the enemy. I think we've got a lot more passion and pride about us than them. We'll definitely show that on the day.'

Those comments came before the Slovakia game, remember, and I recall speaking to many fans in Bordeaux who said 'You know what, he's right, we do have more passion, and tomorrow is our chance to prove it'. You saw in the last chapter how we did in that regard: we blew Europe into next week with our passion in that game – I firmly believe that – and that trend continued as the games rolled on and more and more people were touched by Wales' magic. The English bit – of course they did – and Hodgson slammed Bale's comments as being disrespectful in his pre-match press conference, but Bale was just being genuine, so what the problem was, I'll never know. Maybe he hit a nerve.

Now, if you're not Welsh, you're probably going to think he's winding England up, saying Wales have more passion, but think about it for a second. How many of England's players belt the anthem out at the start of every game like their lives depend on it? How many of them know all of the words? How many times do England fans spontaneously sing the anthems in games to pick their team up? How many times does their star player come off the pitch with cramp after running his arse off against a supposedly better team in order to hold on for a victory? I've come up with those examples in ten seconds, and Wales players and fans have done all of those things – I can't remember many English fans or players doing the same in the last few years. The defining image for me of England's players and fans interacting was Wayne Rooney saying 'Nice to see your own fans booing you! If that's what loyal support is...' after his side drew their opening game against the USA in South Africa six years ago. You can go on and on and on, but for me, Bale's not wrong at all. Bale said we'd show it on the day, and we did. Wales' ticket allocation for that game in Lens was like being in an away crowd at Old Trafford – we were totally outnumbered, but we belted our anthem out and hardly heard a peep from the English until the second half.

wwAndrew Gwilym noted that one of Bale's answers in a press conference was his standout moment of the tournament: 'You get a lot of bluster out of footballers sometimes, but when he sat down and said he thought Wales could win against England, you didn't think he was messing – he absolutely meant it, he genuinely believed it. I just think that mindset, that approach, it just rubs off on everyone. I can remember asking him two days before the England game if he could put into words what it meant to put on the Wales shirt. He just looked at me and said it means everything to him – to have that dragon on his chest makes him feel fantastic and ten feet tall. I left that room feeling ten feet tall having heard him say that, and the way he answered that question I'd have wanted to go and play ninety minutes with him, so I don't know what it did to the people in that dressing room. I'll always remember being in that press conference room and listening to Gareth Bale say that, because it totally resonated with how I feel to be Welsh and how I'd feel if I was wearing that jersey. He was a real all-round leader – he's not captain, and he's nowhere near the only leader in that group either, but the example he sets is so potent and it does something to people.'

It did do something to people. Again I go back to the fact that these Welshmen were just so genuine and blatantly out there to enjoy themselves and fulfil the nation's pride that it was infectious. Everyone was talking about Bale, Ramsey, Coleman, Williams et al., because their confidence and authenticity was captivating the nation. They were happy to sit there and answer questions about anything and everything, right down to who was winning in the table tennis in any given week. This was in stark contrast to the English press, who were struggling to get any noteworthy insight out of the likes of Ross Barkley, as one English journalist told me, expressing their incredulity at the fact that Gareth Bale was Wales' most regular press conference interviewee up to that point. Dinard just seemed to bring the best out of everyone, though. The media centre there was like a shrine to Welsh football, with '#TogetherStronger' flags draped from the ceilings, pictures of the team everywhere, plenty of space and a stage for those speaking in press conferences to perform on. It was just immaculate – there were separate TV studios, a room for the written press to do interviews, a canteen for everyone... It was perfect, as Rob Dowling noted. 'We flagged it up as being important from the very start, because obviously with the number of journalists and broadcasters that would be coming along, we realised how important it was to make them feel welcomed and wanted there, to give them a comfortable working environment. We wanted people to come there and see what we were all about, see our branding, see our personalities and so on. We didn't want that initial moment of them coming in to be negative, so that we didn't set a negative tone with regards to stories.'

You didn't have to be Welsh for it to do something to you. Earlier we touched on how important the team base of Dinard was, and the players were welcomed back to the town as if they were royalty after every single game, with crowds of people gathering and performing for the Dragons on their return to the team hotel. Owain Fôn Williams recalled: 'Coming back to Dinard after the game was an incredible experience every time we went back there. Fair play to them, they really bought into us and welcomed us with songs or dancing every time we came back, they were there constantly to support us. They even mimicked the Icelandic clapping at one point! They were fantastic – they made us feel so welcome, and it definitely played a massive part towards how successful we were in the tournament.'

Nothing was ever going to live up to Bordeaux, and Lille (where my friends and I decided to base ourselves before the England game in Lens), on this occasion at least, didn't even come close. Whilst Wales were scheduled to take on England in Lens on the 16th, Russia faced off against Slovakia in Lille on the 15th and, since practically every Welsh and English fan had followed our lead and based themselves in Lille for the Lens clash, the whole group found themselves camped in the city for the two games – Russian, Slovak, Welsh and English fans... and it certainly made for an interesting atmosphere.

Whereas the Welsh and the Slovaks had got on like best friends in Bordeaux, there had been some incredibly upsetting scenes down in Marseille, where England had taken on Russia in their first game of the group. Russian Ultras had viciously assaulted English fans, throwing chairs, flares and pipes, and going around in packs attacking the English. It was unbelievable to see, and just ruined the jovial atmosphere that Wales had been used to up to that point. Sure, most of these Ultras had been arrested since then, but there was still a fair bit of trouble in Lille as some English fans still had an axe to grind and clashed again with the Russians, as well as the police, on the night before the game in Lens. The Welsh and the English got on really well, mind, rather surprisingly – although who knows if that would have happened if it hadn't been for everyone fearing the Russians.

On a personal level, there were still a few good memories – basically bringing Lille to a standstill being one. We had a kick-about outside Flandres train station that initially started out as just a few of us having fun, but ended up with the whole square of about 150–200 of us kicking the ball into the air over and over, to see who'd be brave enough to head it back up again. Simple things for simple minds and whatnot. We also had a game with a French-Algerian lad who supported Portugal – who even tried to model himself on Ronaldo and everything, as you do – and I jokingly said to him we'd see him again in the quarter-finals (thinking Portugal and ourselves would win our respective groups and go on to reach that stage)... I didn't quite get that one right, but there we are!

On the day of the game itself, everything was pretty perfect, to be honest. The Russians, having been beaten by the Slovaks the day before, seemed to have mostly disappeared, and the Welsh and English were still in good spirits and ready for the biggest game of the group stages. Inflatable sheep were flying about, everyone was chanting, getting on, dancing – all was as it should have been. There appeared to be a few more English fans about than Welsh fans, but nowhere near as many as it turned out to be once we'd all got into the stadium. People were scrambling for taxis and haggling for cheaper seats on the trains to the stadium, but I don't think any of us realised just how isolated a place Lens was and maybe that was why so many people were struggling to get there – nonetheless, when everyone arrived, we'd soon liven the place up.

Kit Symons, former Wales assistant manager and newly reappointed to the Welsh coaching staff, was out in France for the whole month doing some scouting work for the team, and he had a particularly interesting experience trying to find his way to the game: 'My standout moment... I flew from Toulouse into Lille, hoping to get into Lens for the England game – but there were no taxis to get me there, so I had to get on some shuttle bus at the airport. Then I bumped into some boys from Barry who had a bus going down to Lens – it was the only way I could get there. They made me take a swig out of this big bottle – it must have been paraffin or something, it was horrible – before they let me on there! That sort of summed up the whole experience, everyone all singing and dancing and enjoying themselves, getting there the only way they could to watch the England game. It was brilliant, it was hilarious. I still owe them €20 to be honest with you, but there we go!' What a guy!

An all-British clash, two British styles of play, and, perhaps fittingly, Lens' Stade Felix-Bollaert was by far the most 'British' of all of the grounds Wales played in. Four completely separate stands, steep walkways, bog standard concourses, exposed concrete everywhere… there had been no effort to make the place look more aesthetically pleasing – it was what it was and that was it, but it was still bloody perfect. Bordeaux was an art-gallery, Lyon and Lille were stunning stadiums draped with crazy metal origami. Lens' stadium was just that: a stadium, a place where a vast number of people could come together and watch an event, and that's what this was – an event, of the very highest order! The stadium was almost synonymous with the game in a sense: in the same way that UEFA hadn't tried to cover up the ground's rough edges, no-one had tried to cover up how they felt about the game. Bale believed Wales would win, and openly said so, while Hodgson felt similarly about England's chances. UEFA had said long before the tournament began that this was going to be the biggest fixture of the group stages – who cares about the stadium? You could have played this match down the park and 40,000 people would still have enjoyed it just as much.

The banter between the Welsh and the English in the town before the game was fantastic, with plenty of songs about sheep being sung by both sets of fans – no need to elaborate further on the content of those songs! – and when we got to the stadium, that looked set to continue as there was no segregation between the supporters inside the ground. It was nowhere near a 50–50 situation, mind, although few were expecting it to be, with the Welsh fans taking up only about a fifth of the stadium in total, maybe less! Having seen their side waste countless opportunities against the Russians and succumb to a late equaliser, the English we were mixing with in the concourse before kick-off weren't feeling confident. Hodgson had opted to go with the same line-up as he had selected to face Russia, with Rooney in midfield and Kane up front to take the corners, whilst Vardy and Sturridge warmed the bench. Wales, meanwhile, welcomed Hal Robson-Kanu and, incredibly, Joe Ledley back to the starting XI after they had come on as subs to change the game against Slovakia. The referee – Felix Brych – was the same man that had officiated Wales' famous 1–0 victory over Belgium in qualification... which some saw as a good omen for the 90 minutes of football that lay ahead of them!

Something that has become quite the opposite in terms of omens is the away kit Wales had to wear against England. Manchester United famously abandoned their grey away strip back in the late 1990s after Sir Alex Ferguson deemed that it was having a negative effect on his players, that they couldn't see each other to pick out passes and so on. Wales are still yet to win in this grey kit, and it became a bit of a hoodoo for fans towards the latter stages of Wales' run at the Euros – players told me that it never got to the point where they felt like they wouldn't win just because they were in that top, but the Team Equipment Manager Dai Griffiths apparently did send a text to someone at the start of the tournament saying the away kit needed to be scrapped, for one reason or another, whether that be visibility or the omens behind it.

People were paying up to £1000 for a ticket to this game, it was totally crazy, and somehow the English had managed to get hold of a good three-quarters of the allocation, leaving our merry little band of Welshmen totally outnumbered. However, as became an unspoken rule throughout the tournament, no matter how outnumbered we were or whatever alcohol- or travel-induced illnesses we were suffering from at the time, we still sang our anthem louder than anyone we came up against. This time though, because we were so outnumbered, and against England, it seemed to have that extra edge to it.

Chris Coleman's team talk didn't alter for the occasion though, as he doesn't usually need to supply extra motivation to get his boys ready for the occasion: 'It was no different than usual, the team talk.' James Chester said. 'The gaffer's team talk before every game is fairly simple, but they're inspirational in the way that they get us all up for the game and wanting to perform to our best – I certainly think that whilst I've been playing for Wales there haven't been too many games where we've turned up and not performed, so that speaks for itself really. Maybe on that day, with it being such a big game, a derby against such big rivals, we'd perhaps been pumped up a little too much and when we did get the ball we weren't calm enough to do what we needed to do with it.'

One thing that became patently obvious straight away was that England knew what they were doing against Wales, more so than any other team the Dragons faced in the tournament. Opponents tended to either sit back and absorb, looking for a counter, or to press very high up the pitch and unsettle Chris Coleman's men. England did the latter, and did so very well indeed. With less than five minutes gone, Ashley Williams made a bit of a mess of a clearance after coming under pressure from Harry Kane, leaving Ben Davies to sweep up once more and relieve the pressure for Wales. Unfortunately, the relief didn't last very long as Hodgson's men soon had the ball back and were shifting it about at quite a pace. Neil Taylor and Chris Gunter probably had one of the most difficult games they've ever had for Wales, as Raheem Sterling and Danny Rose doubled up on Gunter, whereas Kyle Walker and Adam Lallana kept Taylor busy on the opposite flank. Soon enough Wales found themselves sitting so deep because of England's possession that they could seldom get out and mount an attack of their own. Aaron Ramsey was a candidate for Wales' man of the match in most games for his attacking play in particular, but here he was exceptional at the defensive end and absolutely tireless in his efforts to keep Wales in the game – by necessity a far cry from the Rambo that would waltz around the pitch with relative ease in the Dragons' better attacking performances in this tournament, thanks to England's relentless pressing.

Davies and Bale had a couple of chances for Wales inside the opening ten minutes, but after that Kane, Rooney and Alli all had chances to put England ahead as England began amassing the 70% possession they'd end up with in the match. The Dragons were battling the Three Lions, and hanging on for dear life at times. White shirts just seemed to be everywhere, but one unbelievable, crazy moment turned what had been an almost entirely one-sided affair up to that point on its head in emphatic fashion. With less than five minutes to go in the first half, Bale was fouled by Rooney around 40 yards from goal, and the Welshman – despite the distance – soon rose to his feet and lined the ball up for an effort on Joe Hart's goal. A ridiculous distance to attempt a shot from – so much so that when the Real Madrid winger did shoot, from my seat at the opposite end of the pitch and with Hart diving low to save the ball, it looked like it had been put out for a corner, yet we still celebrated, such was the difficulty for Wales to get any offensive foothold in the match. The reality was far more exhilarating; incredible in truth – Joe Hart would call himself a villain after the game for conceding the goal, but he was probably as close as an England player can get to being a hero to Wales fans after the monumental cock-up he made in attempting to save Bale's effort from such a ludicrous distance. 1–0 TO WALES, ABSOLUTELY UNBELIEVABLE!

Sharing an unsegregated stand with the English in that moment was interesting, especially with a couple of England fans penned in amongst thousands of Welsh fans – we were hugging stewards, ripping shirts; jumping on seats, railings, everything. To go ahead was just insane after the half we'd had, but even media professionals were affected by the scenes, as Owain Tudur Jones would note: 'The guys at S4C wanted the cameras rolling in the studio throughout the game, so they could see myself and Dylan (Ebenezer) reacting to anything that happened. I actually stepped out to watch most of the England game just to soak it all in because, as much as people criticise England and give them stick, I enjoyed seeing the power of England as a nation and how many of their fans had tickets to the game. When Bale scored the free-kick, I ran back into the studio – too late to get the good footage of celebrating – but in the meantime, Dylan had gone absolutely insane, I think. There was water, coffee, sweets getting thrown about, flying everywhere – having seen the footage back, his face was an absolute picture – just the pure look of shock on his face!' Some of the British media after the match said that Wales losing to England was humiliating, but to be fair the most humiliating thing to me was seeing the English boo their players off the pitch at half-time – these guys were dominating the game almost completely, and had only gone behind thanks to a goalkeeping howler, really, yet here the fans were, booing their own team.

One of the defining images of the tournament for me came when walking down to the concourse at half-time. At the bottom of a long, single flight of stairs was one set of delirious, hot, sweaty fans, jumping up and down and throwing their arms about, relentlessly singing 'Don't take me home'… whereas further down the concourse there was another bunch of fans walking around glumly, heads down, probably wanting to sing 'Please take me home.' Which ones were the Welsh fans, do you think? That went on, non-stop for the entire half-time break, and the Welsh fans' singing continued uninterrupted into the second half while the English fans didn't seem too interested… until they equalised. Having drawn their first game 1–1 with Russia, losing 1–0 to Wales in this game would have surely meant the chop for Hodgson – although it did get to that point anyway, in the end – so he had to respond, and bringing Jamie Vardy and Daniel Sturridge on at half-time wasn't a bad way to do that. Ben Davies would admit to me after the tournament that he believed Wales were somewhat guilty of being too content to defend at times during the match, and at this point, with Vardy, Sturridge, Rooney and Alli launching attack after attack after attack, it seemed inevitable that England would equalise soon.

When it did come, through Vardy in the 56th minute, there was no groaning from the Welsh – just shouting louder, singing the anthem, keeping the support up. The players didn't panic and weathered the English storm until injury time, though not creating anything of note of their own. 'I think the way the game panned out was as expected – we knew all the pressure was on them, and we were quite happy to let them have the ball, but the most disappointing thing from our perspective was when we had the ball,' James Chester said. 'We didn't play to our identity and the way we played in the qualifiers, where we were beating teams. I think had we done that then we'd have caused England a lot of problems on the break, if we'd taken more care on the ball.'

The ultimate sucker-punch came in added time. With Sturridge sneaking into the box, Chris Gunter slipping and then a gap opening up at Wayne Hennessey's near post as the keeper's vision was obstructed by the stumbling Gunter, the Liverpool striker prodded home for a 91st-minute winner. The celebrations after that goal were a perfect demonstration of how far Wales had come under Chris Coleman though – the English fans were suddenly singing their heads off, as they knew there had been a point when they had been very likely to lose this game. With just seconds of added time left to play, all of that pressure was suddenly gone.

The way Gary Neville ran all the way down the touchline from the dugout to celebrate with the England players in the corner really got to some of the Wales players. Team Performance Psychologist Ian Mitchell explained: 'The England game was emotional for a number of reasons. We were outnumbered and I felt it as soon as we went out. There was a massive England crowd, a helicopter right above us throughout the warm-up and I think we did come away from our focus slightly in the game, and you could tell because the possession was down massively. We didn't play very well for a number of reasons, and emotionally it was a big distraction – for whatever reason. Maybe because players were against people that they knew, that they were friends with... because a lot of them came into our dressing room after the game and were chatting with our boys, so it was a very different game for a number of reasons.'

The Welsh fans applauded their players – most of whom were absolutely spent from all the running they'd done – before Gareth Bale got them all together for their customary post-match huddle, where captain Ashley Williams said a few very important words. It was an incredible attitude from the entire group, considering that stinging feeling of conceding an injury-time goal – and the game – to your biggest rivals was so raw, but the reaction that set social media and

Welsh hearts alight came shortly afterwards when the players had finished their huddle. 'Once that goal went in and the whistle went, players and fans do go through different emotions.' Chris Gunter said. 'We knew at that time that it was a massive kick in the stomach for us, and I remember looking at the screen with two or three minutes to go and there was a guy in the Welsh end crying. I'm assuming he was thinking it would have been a good result for us to hang onto the draw and stay top with four points – we were all thinking that – then obviously we concede. As players, we need the fans to help get us through, but never really do you see players lifting the fans. It just seemed natural at that time that I should go and try and lift them. If I hadn't been playing, I'd have been in that Welsh end anyway and absolutely devastated at what just happened, and maybe to see a player go over and say "Keep your heads up, because it's not over. Even though this really hurts, we've got another game in a few days and we can still do it!" I just thought if it could lift one or two of them then it'd be worth doing, and maybe it did work slightly!'

There were many moments of inspiration throughout this incredible journey for Wales – not just in the tournament, but in qualifying too – and (*SPOILERS*) there are still plenty more to come, but this moment, with Chris Gunter going over to the thousands of devastated Welsh fans and gesturing to them to keep their chins up going into the third and final group game against Russia, was up there with any of them and certainly had the effect Chris intended. It went some way to proving Bale's point from his pre-match press conference, too, about the passion, the unity and the spirit shared by this group of players and their incredibly dedicated disciples. However, speaking of proving points, having departed from their usual style of play somewhat after the emotion and the circus of the England game, Chris Coleman's men certainly had a few to prove going into their final game against Russia in Toulouse four days later!

Standings after Matchday 2

Pos.	Team	GP	W	D	L	F	A	GD	Pts.
1	England	2	1	1	0	3	2	1	4
2	Wales	2	1	0	1	3	3	0	3
3	Slovakia	2	1	0	1	3	3	0	3
4	Russia	2	0	1	1	2	3	- 1	1

Results

England 2–1 Wales

Russia 1–2 Slovakia

CHAPTER 5

Russia vs Wales

Stadium de Toulouse – 20 June 2016

'Nights like tonight when you see your supporters...
As a nation, geographically we're small.
But for heart, we were a continent tonight.'

CHRIS COLEMAN, WALES MANAGER

'I THINK THAT defeat came at the perfect time for
Wales – it just gave them a wake-up call, a timely
reminder that they can't go out there and be negative
or try and sit back. They need to go out and try to
get themselves on the front foot from the first minute
to the last.' Those were the words of former Wales
international Jack Collison after the England game,
but a wake-up call is one thing – how do you pick
yourself up for another game four days after a defeat
like that against your biggest rivals?

Chris Gunter had done all anyone could ever need
to do to lift the supporters' spirits with his fantastically
simple gesture after the game, and Neil Taylor detailed
how the players picked themselves up immediately
after the final whistle, using the disappointment of

the English defeat to drive them on to prove a point against Russia. 'It was just like usual, we always stick together whether we win, lose or draw. It was just a case of "Right, listen: f*** it. We did our best, the best we could – we worked hard and stuck together. It didn't work, and we just go again." It's as simple as that: there's no blame-game or anything like that. It doesn't exist in our team, not with Wales, and we all feel bad when we lose and great when we win. The Welsh fans were still the loudest, by far, despite how few of them had managed to get tickets. They were the loudest throughout the match until England got that second goal. They were the best set of fans in the tournament and I think the England celebrations after they got that late winner says a lot. That drove us on – the fact that Gary Neville ran all the way down the touchline to celebrate too – it pushed us on to respond and make sure we got out of that group.'

Returning to Dinard after the game, the location and its people further endeared themselves to the Welsh squad as there were little messages littered around the hotel for the players and the staff, telling them that the people were still proud of the team regardless of what had just happened against England. This was massively appreciated by everyone involved, but once you're back there, what do you do? Preparation for the next game against Russia would get going the day after Wales returned to their little Tenby-en-France home from home, but on that first day back there was a bit of uncertainty regarding the itinerary for the day. The coaching staff had planned to give the players the day off to do whatever they wanted – to spend time with families, keep themselves to themselves, whatever they fancied. However, the players had other ideas. Gareth Bale, Joe Ledley and the other senior players went to the coaches and said that they wanted everyone to stay together, to recover together, relax together and then go out for food together – that's what they felt they needed to do to pick themselves up for the third and final group game.

The most disappointing thing for all involved after the England game was how the players had failed to stick to the team identity that had got them to that point. They had played fairly negative, at times panicky, football against England, rather than the calm, coherent style of powerful transition football that had earned them the privilege of contesting the Euro 2016 group stages in the first place. Neil Taylor detailed how the manager got his side back on point in the days building up to the Russia game. 'The gaffer had a meeting with us. We talked on a few things, watched a few clips of the game where we didn't do as well as we usually would do in certain scenarios, but he just said "Listen boys, the way you played –the occasion might have got to you etc., but if you're going to go out of this tournament, make sure you don't go out of it playing like this, because you'll regret it for the rest of your life. You have to play the way we've always played. Show confidence, be bold on the ball – which we weren't often enough against England – and if it still goes wrong, at least you can still hold your head up high." He gave us that confidence, he showed us loads of clips of where we'd played well and made sure we all remembered how good we were, because when you lose you have to turn it around quickly – especially in tournaments – and the gaffer and the staff were exceptional in helping us do that.'

With England out of the way and no trouble whatsoever in Toulouse from the Russians, the nerves disappeared. The city itself was beautiful, a bit wet at times but the weather picked up soon enough, and Super Furry Animals performed there a few nights before the game itself, which was absolutely crazy. The upcoming fixture felt like Bordeaux 2.0, except this time we had the experience of already winning one game behind us. This meant that we were as good as through, whether that would be in first, second or third, given that Slovakia and England were facing each other in the group's other fixture and at least one of them was going to drop points. Also, any Welsh fan who had been sober enough to actually take in England's game against Russia – so probably not many – knew that England should have smashed the Russians. There were holes all over the place that Roy Hodgson's men got into, but failed to make the most of. If we got Ramsey and Bale into the same spots then we'd absolutely terrorise the opposition in Toulouse.

The Russians made one crucial mistake in the build-up to the game. Yes, they were ravaged by injuries as a side – before the tournament even began, in fact, as they were missing five or six certain starters due to injury – but that was out of their control. What was in their control was the choice of kits, and they let Wales wear the fabled red jersey that would become synonymous with the success of the Dragons in this tournament. That kit carries its own aura and brings something special out of everyone, whether it be players or fans – some fans who had worn the grey away kit to the England game to match the kit the team would wear said they felt out of place not wearing red. There's nothing in it, of course – it's just a psychological thing – but in that sense Russia had handed us a huge advantage in letting us wear the red strip.

With one celebrating his 34th birthday on the day of the game in Toulouse, and the other a 6"+ tree who was verging on 37 years old, the two Russian centre backs weren't going to have much pace about them. Wales could have an absolute field day in transition if they had many opportunities to counter-attack. The usual ploy of using Hal Robson-Kanu as a lone forward to draw defenders and create space didn't seem to be prudent in these circumstances. Many felt that Sam Vokes would be a better choice, with his hold-up play, serious strength and ability to ping the ball off to an onrushing Ramsey or Bale, who could capitalise on already being in their stride while Vokes kept the defenders fairly stationary with his presence.

'On a personal note, to be part of the tournament was brilliant, but I'd missed out on featuring in the first two games so after the manager pulled me to one side before the game and told me I'd be starting, I was buzzing,' Sam Vokes said. 'When we got down to Toulouse and you saw the buzz around the place with all of the support that had travelled down there, it was amazing.' Vokes went on to detail the instructions Chris Coleman had given him. 'I was brought in to hold the ball up, link in with Gareth and Aaron as they ran in behind, and play off them really – it was an ideal game for me, because the two of them were making so many runs past me that we had a lot of fortune from those situations.' Russia couldn't possibly compete in terms of pace, so from their point of view this should have been a tight game where they sat in, tried to absorb Wales' pressure, let Vokes offload the ball into a Bale or a Ramsey buried in traffic, then countered, but it didn't pan out like that at all.

In a throwback of a stadium that was befittingly nicknamed the Mini Wembley because of its uncanny similarity to the original Wembley Stadium in London – right down to the makeshift Wembley Way leading up to the 30,000-seater venue itself – the Russians would not live up to the occasion of a decisive group game on a beautiful night in a heavenly city in the south of France, which could have seen either team go through. No, Russia would be eviscerated, thanks to their poor tactics, lack of discipline and borderline lack of respect for Wales on the night. I say lack of respect because for all any Welshman wants to say against England for whatever reason, at least they did their homework on us and acted upon it when they came up against Coleman's side in Lens. Russia hadn't done their homework, or if they had then their players had fallen asleep in the team meeting, because from the very first kick of a ball they played right into Wales' hands. At the heart of all of Wales' success in the game were the usual suspects, but particularly Joe Allen.

George Best once said that he'd been compared to countless players over the years but that only when they labelled Cristiano Ronaldo 'the next George Best' had it been a compliment to him. Go and show Xavi or Andrea Pirlo or whoever you like what Allen did to Russia, and throughout the tournament in fact, for Wales and ask them if he is their heir apparent, and they should say 'No, this guy's streets ahead of me right now.' He was that bloody good in this tournament, and never more so than in this game. People who don't watch Wales very often, or just hear about them on the news, may assume that Gareth Bale gets chance after chance after chance from cutting inside on his left foot from the right flank and shooting at goal – these are probably the same people who still toot the one-man-team horn. In fact that almost never happens because everybody knows he's going to do it – apart from in this game, where Bale had an opportunity exactly like that after just 57 seconds, with Allen providing the assist. 57 seconds in and you've let the opposition's best player get a run at your defence, pretty much unchallenged at any point, cut inside onto his favoured foot and bang a shot at goal? Igor Akinfeev was equal to it, but this is a guy who was once considered to be the next best thing in goal, and although he had that save in his locker, even he could only spill the ball before making an excellent recovering save to block Sam Vokes' follow-up effort.

You can understand nerves being at fault for the opening lapse that allowed Bale to cut in and do what he did, but the Welsh onslaught just kept on coming as Russia piled men forward to try and chase an opening goal. To do that against Wales – who would prove their prowess in transition against much stronger teams later in the tournament – was absolutely criminal. Russia could well have scored in the game, given the number of players they had in the Wales half trying to create a chance, but if they made even the slightest mistake and lost possession, they were done. The minute Russia slipped up, Neil Taylor, Chris Gunter and Joe Allen immediately tore up the pitch to give Bale, Ramsey and Vokes dozens of chances to put Wales ahead. Wales were viciously quick, going from winning the ball back in their own half to creating a good chance at the other end in the blink of an eye. Ledley or the defenders would win the ball deep, move it quickly into space where Allen or the wing backs were usually waiting to get going, and give Russia a ferocious boot out of the tournament.

'I don't think, looking back, that it's a game you get too often in your career. We knew, very early on to be honest, that we were going to win that game because Russia had set up in a very attacking way, which suited us perfectly with the players we had on the park.' James Chester said of the way Russia chose to play against Wales. 'We performed much better in certain aspects than we did against England, certainly when we had the ball, and we took full advantage of that. It was a very enjoyable night!' After just five minutes, everyone seemed pretty certain that Wales were going to win this. They were just leaving the Russians with their heads spinning, thanks to their blistering intensity, their pace, their incision when moving the ball and their overall superiority. Vokes was a total pain in the backside for the defenders: getting in their faces, making his present felt, backing into them and making them work for every inch of territory they could get – which wasn't much – while all around them the likes of Bale, Ramsey and the wing backs were tying the rest of the Russians up in knots.

The goal soon came, and what a goal it was – symbolic of everything Wales did right in the game. A very hopeful ball played forward on a break from

Russia was intercepted on the halfway line by James Chester, who could only touch the ball into the path of Joe Allen. It was four-on-four as Russia had again piled forward without any thought for the consequences, so Allen advanced forward under no pressure. One defender was standing way off the Welsh Pirlo, one was on Vokes, one was in no-man's-land, and one had his work cut out for him trying to watch Bale on the left wing and Ramsey in the middle. When his head turned, Ramsey broke on the inside of him and the ball Allen played to find Wales' number 10 was absolutely exquisite. The dinked finish from Rambo – one-on-one with Akinfeev – was equally superb, and Wales were in the lead after nine minutes. The whole move from Wales took something like four seconds! It was blisteringly quick, and showed how ruthless Wales were able to be in the game, thanks in no small part to the tactics of the opposition. Some of the Russian players threw their hands up after the ball hit the back of the net as if it was against the run of play, but they'd been thrashed up to that point and Wales were well worthy of their lead.

However, it didn't stop there! 1–0 up after nine minutes with the game already seeming like it had been won – what the hell was happening!? Reading this, if you haven't seen the game, you'll be thinking 'Well, every team has their spell, and Russia's will come'. But on the day it felt like that period had been and gone for them, in the nine minutes where they'd

The calm before the storm. The squad that would take Wales deep into the latter stages line up for a pre-tournament photo in Dinard.

Chris Coleman getting his point across to his squad at the team's training base.

The stunning pre-match display gave fans inside Bordeaux's beautiful stadium goosebumps – we'd reached the promised land before a ball was even kicked.

A total takeover – the Nouveau Stade de Bordeaux rammed with red as over 25,000 Welsh fans filled the stands.

Facing Slovakia the day after Chris Coleman's birthday, is this a Saturday Night Fever impression or Tactical Instructions – maybe both?

James Chester and Ben Davies were excellent throughout the tournament – here's the former, impressing against Slovakia.

BAAAAAALE! Wales score their first European Championship goal with their first shot on target, thanks to that man Gareth Bale!

Hal Robson-Kanu came on to score the goal that saw Wales become the first British team to win their opening game at the European Championships.

A symphony of perfection: Welsh fans create an absolutely joyous racket after securing a 2–1 victory over Slovakia in their opening game.

The legends were out in force in France – Craig Bellamy was spotted in Bordeaux, but my Wrexham-supporting friends and I got a quick snap with Rushy!

After the England match: 'Keep your heads up, because it's not over. Even though this really hurts, we've got another game in a few days and we can still do it.'

After the gutting loss to England, these Dragons felt they had a massive point to prove against Russia in Toulouse for the final group game.

Taylor's on fire, your defence is terrified! If we hadn't seen it, we perhaps wouldn't have believed it, but Tayls scored his first Wales goal in France!

Chris Gunter and Aaron Ramsey celebrate after securing an emphatic victory over Russia to top Group B.

The looks on their faces say it all – Wales topped the group!

With his shoulder somewhat battered, Dragons Captain Ashley Williams gets a hug from Gareth Bale after Wales manage a hard 1–0 victory over Northern Ireland.

'I've seen him on many a dancefloor, but I'm so glad he's brought it to the world finally' – Jack Collison (and many other people)'s highlight of the tournament.

Seeing the players with their children on the pitch after Northern Ireland was such an endearing moment, it made everyone quite emotional.

'The Dragon on my shirt, that's all I need!' Not just a match-winner on the pitch, Bale helped score a few points off of it with his passion in press conferences.

The fans paid homage to Speedo in every game, singing songs and flying flags. He'd have been exceptionally proud of Chris Coleman and the team.

After being in a sling for five days, our battling captain belted a header into the Belgian net for the equaliser in Lille.

What it meant to be back on level terms against the Red Devils – but the comeback didn't stop there…

Hal Johan Kanu with the best goal Wales have ever scored, nailing a Cruyff turn before slotting home for a 2–1 lead.

'I felt like a fan at that point!' Sam Vokes channels his inner Toshack to power Wales into a 3–1 lead.

A standing ovation from the Red Wall in Lille – an incredible trip to the semi-finals in Lyon awaited.

All for the Dragon on their shirts.

Paying tribute to their fellow underdogs, the Dragons mimic Iceland's Thunderclap after securing victory over Belgium in the quarter-finals.

The Godfather of
Welsh Football,
everybody – Mark
Evans!

Truer words
have never been
spoken. Joe Allen
was superb for
Wales and made
UEFA's Team of
the Tournament.

Speaking to BBC Radio Cymru with some good friends in Lyon, the afternoon before Wales took on Portugal in the semi-finals of Euro 2016.

The journey had to end somewhere. The Red Wall shows its undiminished appreciation for their heroes after being knocked out by Portugal.

The Dragons thanked us, but we'll never be able to thank them enough for the memories they gave us over the course of this past summer.

had their brief moments attacking Wales before being countered and beaten back into their shells. The Russians weren't coming back into this one now, or at least that's how we all felt.

Ten minutes later it was all but confirmed, thanks to perhaps the most unlikely of goal-scorers for Wales. Even Wayne Hennessey had scored for Wales before, when he put away a free-kick against Turkey for the under-19s, but the scorer of the second goal against Russia was getting his first ever goal for the Dragons at any level, and you could see on his jubilant little face just how happy he was to score. Yes, Neil Taylor scored his first ever goal for Wales against Russia – after two bites at the cherry, mind – and the manager and the squad playfully mocked him for it the next day, bless him, such is the fantastic bond and banter amongst the squad. 'We had a laugh about it in the hotel the next day –the gaffer put a video of it up on the screen. He had a little laugh, pausing it on my face, and said I looked like a little kid who'd just nicked sweets from the candy shop, or something like that. I got wound up about it a lot, but it was great – it was brilliant. But my main memory of that game was that we played so well, we were so comfortable and we'd started playing the way we needed to again. We made hundreds of passes, and the fans were singing every song they knew.'

'Tayls' also recalled the goal vividly. 'It was one of them where I was hoping Bale would slip me in, but if he'd played it I'd have been just a tad offside. But they attacked, and myself and Gunts broke straight away once we had the ball back – it's hard to keep up with Gareth most of the time, mind... I wasn't going to shoot, because I knew Vokesy was there somewhere to my side, so I was planning to square it to him. But the defender was covering the angle so I had to shoot. I tried to put it through the keeper's legs, didn't happen, so I just put my foot through it the second time.'

Again, the goal showed how awful Russia were. As Bale led a break in transition – yet again capitalising on Russia's unwise attacking tactics – the defenders all seemed to magnetise to him, Ramsey and Vokes, who were making moves in the centre of the pitch. Their right back and centre back were both marking Vokes at one point, leaving acres of space for Taylor to burst through totally unchallenged. He did very well to stay onside, but once he did he found himself on his own in the box – six Russian players all chasing back, wondering how he'd got beyond them – before firing straight at Akinfeev, who parried, allowing Taylor to put away the rebound. He ran off to celebrate in front of a crowd who were pretty much all thinking the same thing: 'Holy shit, we're dominating and we're going through to the last 16!'

With the greatest respect in the world to Taylor, at this point we were all wondering if there was something in the water down south that was making us hallucinate, but no, we were all living our wildest dreams and Wales were 2–0 up after 20 minutes and – given that England were still level with Slovakia – top of the group on six points from two games. 'I think myself and Ash at the back were probably two of the most shocked men in the stadium when we saw Neil had gone through and scored,' James Chester said after seeing Taylor busting the net on the half-volley, before noting how it perfectly paid tribute to the importance of the wing backs: 'He took a bit of stick off us all for the next couple of days how he went about it finishing it off, but I think it summed up how important he and Gunter were on that night and throughout the tournament. Not just defensively, but getting forward in support too – but the way Russia set up in that game definitely helped us along the way.'

In truth, it could have been 4–0 at half-time to Wales, such was the free rein Russia were giving to Allen, Ramsey and Bale. You naturally begin to ask questions as to whether Wales were doing so well because they were performing out of their skins, or if Russia were just abysmal. It was a bit of both, to be honest, and the second half continued in the same manner as the Dragons totally torched Russia's hopes of escaping Toulouse with anything to show for their time there. Four minutes into the second half, Aaron Ramsey found Chris Gunter (in a separate post code to the Russians who were supposed to be marking him) with a dissecting ball that gave the wing back plenty of time to put a cross in for Vokes. A lucky deflection from the defender saw the ball go behind for a corner, but it showed Wales had more than picked up where they left off in the first half. Ramsey and Bale were at it again minutes later, from defence to attack in a flash, with only Akinfeev's foot stopping Wales going three up. After 67 minutes Wales did get their third, and it was Gareth Bale who got it, dinking over Akinfeev from an angle after a beautiful through ball from Ramsey. The Russians just looked at each other in disbelief, as if this hadn't been coming – or maybe they couldn't believe that they'd only just gone three down after having lumps knocked out of them by Wales from the very first minute – and the Welsh fans celebrated in the same manner.

3–0 up with 20 minutes to go, your team passing the ball around under no pressure and chanting with every successful pass – at the time we all thought this was as good as it got. That night for us, watching that performance, was the moment we all felt that Wales could go some way in this competition. If Wales kept playing like this, even against better opposition, it was going to take an awful lot to knock them out of the tournament, and that prospect in the long term excited all of us beyond belief. Whereas Wales had lost control against England, they had it in abundance against a hideously undisciplined Russian side – a side that at times didn't look like they'd graduated from Sunday League level. Before that, though, the short-term success that we were about to achieve was unthinkable. England were still level with Slovakia, so Wales were still top of the group.

Before the tournament, if you'd asked the fans what they thought they'd be doing in the last 20 minutes of their final group game, many of them would have probably told you something about reminiscing over the beauty of the journey they'd been on; that goal they'd scored in the game they nearly won; how proud they were of the boys for giving everything they had out on the pitch; that they'd learn from the experience going forward as the third-placed team – something along those lines. None would have said they'd have been *olé*-ing Welsh passes for twenty minutes straight whilst watching the English throw away the top spot. Wales' Dragons were about to claw that away from them in emphatic fashion, after becoming the first British team to win their opening game, the highest first-half scorers in the tournament up to that point – and the host of other records and personal ambitions that were realised on the journey thus far. Every little experience up to this point had just left fans shaking their heads in disbelief, and there'd be many more moments like that going forward. England may have won the battle, but we won the war, as Wales unbelievably snatched top spot with an emphatic 3–0 win.

'Someone wrote that we'd walked the international stage as if we'd been there for years, not as if we were there for the first time, so that says it all really,' said Ian

Gwyn Hughes, the FAW's Head of Communications. 'You just felt that maybe Russia were due one really good performance, but the other thing that was in our favour was that Russia had to win. They had to come at us, and if teams do that then we can cut anyone to shreds. You watch players play with Wales ... you see the performances of Chris Gunter, Ben Davies, James Chester, Sam Vokes, Jonny Williams, and you just wonder why they're not starting every week for their clubs. Joe Allen too – why wouldn't Liverpool build a team around him, the way he plays? The only ones who didn't play at all were George Williams, David Cotterill, David Vaughan and Owain Fôn Williams, yet not once did any of them complain – they just kept supporting and wanting the journey to last for as long as it possibly could. To get the best out of these players as we did, and to keep the squad as united and as happy as it is, takes great management skills – and that says a lot for Chris Coleman and his talents as a manager.'

If ever Coleman gets bored of working in football then he should definitely turn his hand to public speaking, because very few people can inspire and motivate people like he did on numerous occasions in qualifying and during the tournament. On this night in particular, his words spoke for the pride of a nation which found itself in dreamland: 'I said there was more to come from this group of players. They're on the way to something else – I'm just glad we're on it with them. We'll have to see who we get next. We'll respect everyone, but we have nothing to fear. Looking at the group, with England, Russia and Slovakia, we knew it was going to be tough, and it was all down to the last game. To win it was great. I'm very proud of the players. We enjoyed tonight, and being at the top of the group is a bonus. The performance was really pleasing. I've been a player myself. I'm so lucky to be experiencing something now as a manager, at a tournament – and to see the team perform like that, it's really pleasing. I'm immensely proud. Nights like tonight, when you see your supporters... As a nation, geographically we're small. But for heart, we were a continent tonight.' That last bit gets me welling up every time – what a bloody perfect thing to say!

Actually, all of it was spot on, but what topped off the post-match celebrations was yet another demonstration of fancy footwork from everyone's favourite bearded one: Joe Ledley! 'I got a bit of stick for saying this the other day. Hal Robson-Kanu's goal was incredible, don't get me wrong, but Joe Ledley's dance moves were the highlight of the tournament for me. What an absolute joy to watch!' Jack Collison said after seeing Ledley dance in front of the thousands of Welsh fans in Toulouse after the Russia victory. 'I've seen him on many a dancefloor over the years, but I'm so glad he's brought it to the world finally and shared it with the fans – it was great to see him enjoying himself so much, and the fans loving every second of it too. Definitely the dancing was the highlight for me!'

For all the talk of the Sweden defeat two weeks earlier and how devastating that would be for Wales, here the Dragons were, going through to the Round of 16 as group winners, whilst Zlatan Ibrahimović's Sweden exited the tournament with their tails between their legs. UEFA's Mark Pitman offered an insight into why the Welsh had been so successful after picking themselves up from that early setback: 'I travelled to and from each game on the team plane, and to have that sort of access in a tournament in which they did so well was an incredible experience. Being with the players privately when their families visited after the games against Russia and Northern Ireland showed a different side to them, being away from the press and public scrutiny. It made you realise the whole '#TogetherStronger' motto isn't just marketing; it's a true reflection of this group, a group of close friends. No stars, just a team that have had dark times playing for Wales, and knew that this tournament offered an opportunity to shine in front of the entire world. I think they did just that.' Wales had certainly done that up to this point, but they had no plans on stopping with Russia as an incredible journey into the knockout rounds opened up before them.

Standings after Matchday 3

Pos.	Team	GP	W	D	L	F	A	GD	Pts.
1	Wales	3	2	0	1	6	3	3	6
2	England	3	1	2	0	3	2	1	5
3	Slovakia	3	1	1	1	3	3	0	4
4	Russia	3	0	1	2	2	6	-4	1

Results

Russia 0–3 Wales
England 0–0 Slovakia

CHAPTER 6

Wales vs Northern Ireland

Parc des Princes, Paris – 25 June 2016

'That's why Gareth is the player he is – when he
got one clear opportunity to deliver something of real
quality, he did it, and that was the only difference.'

MICHAEL O'NEILL, NORTHERN IRELAND MANAGER

JUST WOW! WHAT else do you say about Wales'
tournament up to this point!? After Sweden, the vast
majority of supporters predicted the Dragons would
struggle to have much of an impact in the Euros.
That's just our pessimistic side, I guess, giving way
to that negativity which has built up over the years.
We need to let that go now – and after what happened
in France this summer, I think we definitely will! On
the other hand, though, before the tournament the
realists among us would have said that Wales' Euro
2016 path would consist of a commendable run in
the group stages, finishing second or third to meet a
heavyweight in the next round, and give them a run
for their money – then come what may, we'd have all
taken that quite happily! Before the tournament, we

had assumed that any last-16 match we got through to would be in Nice after finishing second to England – probably facing Portugal or Austria and trying our luck to get to the quarter-finals against France. Suddenly everything was different. We had just eviscerated Russia (who almost everyone was probably guilty of overestimating) with one of the performances of the tournament. More importantly, this next match was supposed to be THE game – this would be where we showed the world what we're made of, where we accepted the odds would be stacked against us going through and would do our best to overcome them regardless. We all know that the underdog tag brings something else out of this team, but after the performance against Russia and the way the draw went for Wales, we didn't have that to fall back on and it changed the complexion of the game.

Our opponents in the Round of 16 would be decided the day after Wales thrashed Russia. For about 80 minutes, it looked like we'd get what we were expecting, because Turkey seemed to be the team that Wales would play against in the next round. Not a heavyweight, but with Arda Turan, Hakan Çalhanoğlu, Nuri Şahin and more quality names lining their squad, it would have been quite easy for Wales to paint the Dragons as the underdogs. Then Robbie Brady scored out of nowhere to put the Republic of Ireland 1–0 up against Italy, pushing Turkey out of contention for a place in Paris. This landed Northern

Ireland, who are a great team – not a heavyweight, but a great team – in Wales' lap for a repeat of the March friendly. Except that this time Wales would have a full complement of talent to choose from and expectations of them were now high, making them the clear favourites in the eyes of the media. Imagine the mixed feelings then, on the way to Paris for this game: on the back of winning – yes, WINNING – our group, we were heading for a knockout-stage match against Northern Ireland in which we were absolutely the favourites, and it just didn't feel right.

The Northern Irish, although more than confident in their own ability, were in some respects initially disappointed to draw Wales. Knowing they were already through before the Republic of Ireland result that ended up pairing Michael O'Neill's men with Chris Coleman's side in Paris, Kyle Lafferty and co. had assumed Italy would secure victory over the Republic, which would have resulted in a tie against France in Lyon for Northern Ireland. This would have been a fantastic occasion for the Northern Irish on so many levels. They would have had an extra day's recovery, they'd have been facing the hosts of the tournament, and the game would have taken place in Lyon, where Northern Ireland were based, so there would be no faffing about organising hotels and moving around and so on – plus they had already beaten Ukraine in that stadium.

It would have been perfect for Northern Ireland,

as O'Neill admitted to me, before detailing how he talked his players out of that initial disappointment and worked on turning the tables on Wales, painting his team as the underdogs against the Dragons. 'It didn't take much to talk them round, to be honest with you, so the next morning we got the players together and made it clear to them: we're playing Wales to get to the quarter-final of a tournament. I said to them, "If you'd offered either team this situation before the tournament, both of us would have gladly taken it." We were under no illusions that it was going to be a very difficult game, but we genuinely felt we had a good chance of getting beyond Wales and into the quarter-finals. It was a case of them being favourites, but it wasn't too difficult for us to paint it that way to the players or to the press either. When you've got Bale and Ramsey in your squad, playing in the form they were in during the tournament, it was easy for me to turn it around and say how difficult it was going to be, blah, blah, blah, all of that – so it was easy for us to be the underdog.'

It was difficult for Wales, because suddenly the expectations totally changed. The scenario was more difficult for the Dragons than it was for Northern Ireland, with O'Neill's side playing off the fact that when they played in the Parc des Princes against Germany they'd only lost 1–0, despite a plethora of attempts on goal in one of the most free-flowing, powerful footballing performances of the tournament from Germany. Thanks to Northern Ireland's clubless hero Michael McGovern between the sticks, the Green and White Army witnessed their team go through as one of the best third-placed teams. This game against Wales was never going to be a more difficult game than that, surely? Given that the Germany match had only been the Thursday before, the Northern Ireland coaches told the players that they needed to look back to that match and accept that playing against Wales wouldn't be as difficult, and that they'd have a real chance to reach the quarter-finals. The experience of having to play the World Champions in the Parc des Princes to get through the group, and then managing to keep Germany pretty much at bay and keep their goal difference competitive enough to get through in third – all of that worked to Northern Ireland's advantage going into the Wales game.

None of this even crossed the minds of Wales fans – everyone was just thinking of the total dissection of Russia from the previous game. Off the back of that game, a few supporters I spoke to were expecting this Northern Ireland encounter to be a 3–0, 4–0 affair, but it was ridiculous to assume such a thing because it completely ignored the context I've just outlined. Owain Tudur Jones concurred, noting how unrealistic Wales fans' expectations for this game were. 'Northern Ireland were the complete opposite to Russia. What happened at that point in the competition, I felt, was that the expectation levels became totally crazy

– after what had happened in the last game, you ask everyone for predictions and these people are saying we're going to beat Northern Ireland by a big margin, which I thought was so unrealistic. We had to be confident because we'd drawn against them a few months prior without Ramsey, Bale or Robson-Kanu, with Joe Allen on the bench, of course, but tactically, there was no way in hell they were going to allow Gareth Bale to have a free role behind the striker like Russia did.'

Naturally, after scoring three goals in three games up to this point in the tournament, Northern Ireland – like every team with any sense – were going to pay special attention to Bale, but rather than man-mark him, they had other ideas about how to stop him. Opponents can't really man-mark him anyway, because Bale's tendency to roam into wherever the space is disrupts the shape of the opposition. However, O'Neill's men played 3–5–1–1 against Wales, and Jonny Evans had full remit to go as tight to Bale as was needed on the left-hand side of their defensive three. This is obviously where Bale likes to play, coming in on his left foot – coming inside onto a right-footed player as well. The Northern Irish also analysed a heat-map of where Bale gets his touches, and it was pretty evident that that left-hand side of the defence was a key area, so they marked it out on the training pitch in the build-up to the game as an area to pay close attention to. With Evans given full licence to come out and meet Bale and mark him as tightly as he felt was necessary on that side, Craig Cathcart had the same mandate on the other side of the defence, although they weren't really expecting Bale to pop up there too much. Furthermore, Northern Ireland also changed the shape of their midfield, with Corry Evans playing as a deeper man to match Aaron Ramsey's runs. The aim was to try to limit his tendency to run beyond the back four, forcing the defence to drop deeper and giving Bale more space to play in front of them, and in fact because Corry Evans was doing such a good job in matching Ramsey, that didn't really happen too often in this match.

Nevertheless, the Wales squad before the game weren't feeling the pressure – or weren't letting on that they were – as Bale himself pointed out in his pre-match press conference. 'We've just come through a massive journey and we've been in some really bad places before – 117th in the world – but now we're in the last 16 of the Euros, so these days are to enjoy, as the other days were not so easy to enjoy. We're taking it all in our stride; the camp is happy. Obviously after the Russia game we enjoyed the moment, we enjoyed that evening… we're just preparing like we always do, bubbly characters in the squad having a joke and a laugh, but doing our serious work when we have to. It's for you to decide who is favourites… For us, we concentrate on ourselves whether we're favourites or not – the tag doesn't matter to us. We all know what we have to do, what we need to do, and we'll be going on the pitch like every other game: to win it.'

Although some members of the squad admitted that it was a strange situation getting their heads around the fact that they would either be going home straight after the game, or staying on for another week, Joe Ledley spoke defiantly about the squad's ambitions for this game against Northern Ireland. 'As players we weren't ready to go home. We didn't want to go home, and we were enjoying it as much as the fans. With the knockout stages, it's one of those where if you lose you are home within two days, but I'm telling you when the boys were all speaking, we were nowhere near ready to go home. We wanted to just keep carrying on and keep going. It was a tough game – we knew it would be because we'd played against them so recently, the pitch was dry again, and it was hard for us – but we just had to deal with it and fight through it.'

Another incredible atmosphere surely aided the Wales team in that fight, although the nerves and the frailty of both teams' hopes of advancing – this being such an even game that many felt could go either way – meant that the crowd was perhaps slightly more subdued than it had been in the previous games. This was also coupled with the fact that the Welsh fans seemed to be scattered around the Parc des Princes, rather than having one corner or stand to themselves as had been the case previously. 'God

Save The Queen' was once again respected by all, thankfully, but then the Green and White Army got on with singing the song they'd really become famous for over the course of the tournament. A parody of the 1990s dance classic, 'Freed from Desire' by Gala, 'Will Grigg's on Fire' was born out of the Northern Irish forward's incredible form for Wigan Athletic, scoring 25 goals on the way to securing the League One title and promotion to the Championship for the Latics. The chant's popularity hit fever pitch during the tournament – particularly when Michael O'Neill's side faced Germany in the group. There were German fans with 'Will Grigg's on Fire' on the back of their shirts, and Mats Hummels swapped shirts with him and brought Grigg into the German dressing room after the game for pictures with the World Champions, despite the fact that this was a player who didn't get onto the pitch at all throughout the tournament. In the Wales vs Northern ireland match, although the atmosphere was somewhat subdued, the fans were incredible yet again. Persistent Northern Irish chants of Grigg's song were met with jovial jeers and whistles, the Dragons fans chanting 'You've only got one song' in response. To be honest, the atmosphere was the main thing of note in an incredibly tense, difficult first half.

Following an opening period where the Welsh had been given more than a run for their money by the men in green, Aaron Ramsey had the net bulging after

20 minutes, tucking home a ball that Sam Vokes did fantastically well to head down into the newly-blond sensation's path. Unfortunately, it was disallowed for offside, and that set the tone for the whole match, really. It took sustained periods of pressure and probing for Wales to create even a half-chance, whereas Northern Ireland created two or three great chances on the break. They were only level at the break thanks to some great covering defending from James Chester in particular, and equally impressive reflexes from Wayne Hennessey in the Welsh goal. Retreating back to the dressing room at half-time, Northern Ireland were full of confidence and felt the win was well within their grasp, as their tactics stifled everything Wales had done so well previously in the tournament. Bale, Ramsey, the wing backs, Joe Allen: they were all well marshalled for the most part in the first half, and something had to change after the break if Wales were to do what was needed of them and snatch the win.

'I think myself and Aaron Hughes could have counted on two hands how many times we touched the ball all game. We didn't see a lot of the ball on the wings at all because all of the play tended to go down the middle – it was quite a scrappy game,' Wales' Neil Taylor observed. 'The pitch is only watered if both teams agree for it to be watered, so with Northern Ireland playing the way they played – direct, physical, playing against another British team – the game was very difficult, the pitch was very dry... if Russia had been one of the best games of the tournament, the Northern Ireland game was one of the worst. It was so tough physically, and Paris was really hot – everything was against playing good, expansive football, which suited them down to the ground, really.'

Dylan Ebenezer waxed lyrical about Northern Ireland's excellent resolve, admitting to being surprised by how long Michael O'Neill's side were able to stick to their game plan of sitting deep and absorbing pressure for. 'Apart from the England game, that's the worst I felt in the tournament watching a game – just the nerves suddenly kicked in. It's ridiculous because we were in the last 16, exactly where we wanted to be, but we had such an unbelievable chance to get through to the next round and what I thought would be our ultimate game in the quarter-final, and you just didn't want to lose that chance when it was so close and probably as achievable as it was ever going to be. Despite everything, losing at that stage would have been painful, and I think you sensed it from the fans, the players and the staff. Northern Ireland played an absolute blinder – you knew exactly what was coming from them, but I had no idea they'd be so effective nor that they'd be able to keep it up for so long! I was very impressed with them and just so thankful that they didn't really have a top striker. The pressure was all on Wales – you can prepare as much as you like and do whatever to try and make yourself ready for the occasion, but when that pressure gets to you it's a funny thing!'

Kyle Lafferty is a good striker, but many don't realise that he'd played fewer than half a dozen games on loan at Birmingham City towards the end of the season, after hardly playing at all for Norwich City before that, so to expect him to come into the Euros and bang the goals in as he'd done in qualifying was somewhat unreasonable. In addition to that, James Chester showed throughout the tournament – but especially in this game – why the legendary Sir Alex Ferguson regretted letting him leave Manchester United a few years ago. The former Old Trafford Academy player was an absolute star at the heart of Wales' defence, alongside the immovable Ashley Williams and the superb Ben Davies.

Substitutions were again what changed the game for Wales, with Hal Robson-Kanu coming on for Sam Vokes and Jonny Williams entering the fray in place of Joe Ledley. This went some way towards upping the tempo of what had been a very pedestrian game up to that point, thanks to Northern Ireland's willingness to sit deep and attempt to break in numbers. Williams in particular was very effective, like a little Jack Russell zigzagging between the tree-like Northern Irish defenders, desperate to exploit any gaps he could find and give the opposition something to think about. Gareth Bale, who had been restricted to one effort from a free kick and a few blocked shots and crosses, proved to have the decisive impact yet again though, as the attacking triumvirate of Ramsey, Bale and HRK combined to score the game's only goal.

With Robson-Kanu backed into the defence and Neil Taylor finding himself on the edge of the Northern Irish box, Ramsey played a ball into the former Reading forward, the defence slowly collapsing in on itself trying to win the ball back. This gave Bale plenty of space, for the first time in the match, to position himself on the left flank and prepare to launch a low cross in towards a packed area. And what a cross it was – low, precise and driven across the six-yard box. Before you knew it, the ball was in the back of the net, and it was Gareth McAuley who had put it there. The best own goal any Welsh fan has ever seen! To be fair, Robson-Kanu was behind McAuley and would surely have tapped it in had McAuley not done so, but what a cross from Bale. 'It shows you at the end of the day that this is why these players are worth what they are worth,' a disappointed Michael O'Neill would tell me. 'That's why Gareth is the player that he is – when he got one clear opportunity to deliver something of real quality, he did it, and that was the only difference between the two sides in the game. You have a player who has that quality and can deliver it, even when he's not at his best and he's not having the impact that he'd like to have, yet he can still deliver a ball of that quality and that's what you need to win these types of games at this level.'

It wasn't so much a roar that followed the goal, but a collective puffing out of the cheeks – nobody wanted extra time or penalties. After that goal went in, nobody thought we'd see it, because if Northern Ireland were going to come and chase the game then Wales were going to have plenty of space to counter and potentially get another goal, so Welsh fans were quite content in the minutes following the goal. That is until the smallest Dragon clattered into one of the biggest and had all of our hearts in our mouths. Ashley Williams, who again had a brilliant game at the heart of the defence, keeping Lafferty quiet for the most part, had clattered into Jonny Williams and both were lying motionless on the floor.

Both soon got to their feet, but Ash, who has had problems with his shoulder before, looked like his arm was hanging off. Everyone was thinking the same thing – his tournament was over. Despite that though, you could still see him shouting at Chris Coleman on the touchline not to ready a substitute, with both gesturing to each other. Former teammate Owain Tudur Jones recalled witnessing the exchange from *Sgorio*'s studio. 'I loved that moment between him and Chris Coleman, when Chris was ready to bring James Collins on to replace him for the last ten minutes. A lot of people criticised Chris afterwards, saying he should have just taken Ash off, almost as if it was player power, but I saw it differently... There was a look in Ash's eyes, screaming, saying he was fine. Chris

Coleman then countered that with the finger coming out and pointing at him, basically saying "You f****** better be!" Hearing those words, maybe that's when James Collins backed off and thought "Right, Ash is going to carry on in this game" – not that he didn't want to come on. I think that moment highlighted their relationship so well – the respect between Ash and Chris Coleman is massive.'

In a game that was all about Wales finding a way, Lord knows how Ashley Williams found a way to carry on with that injury – it looked gruesome, but it just characterised the spirit and immense determination of the squad. He could quite easily have given up, gone off for James Collins and gone home to rest his shoulder whilst the squad carried on without him, much like Ben Davies could have left Hamšík to dip Ward in the first game against Slovakia. Many other, lesser players would have , but not these Wales players; and that's one of the biggest reasons why Chris Coleman's Dragons were so successful in this tournament. Full time, and the relief poured out of everyone in red as Wales were through to... wait for it... THE QUARTER-FINALS, against Belgium no less!

On an adventure full of beautiful moments, sights and sounds, though, perhaps the most touching of them all came after the final whistle, when the players took to the pitch with their families to celebrate the win and thank the Welsh fans for making the trip in immense numbers once more. Gareth Bale's three-year-old daughter, Alba Violet, did what her father has done so many times, and stole the show by running rings around (and away from!) one of Wales' favourite Princes. She scored a goal in front of the Red Wall before being carried off by Bale, both wearing beaming smiles, and high-fiving UEFA's SpiderCam on her way off the pitch. Incredible scenes, especially getting to see the human side of these people we so often think of as machines, and to see them enjoying the company of their families on this incredible stage that very few of us had ever dreamed our country would reach in our lifetimes. But here we were, with another game in front of our Dragons on their Euro 2016 odyssey.

There was one more celebration to come for Wales before that clash against Belgium though, and it attracted some unfair criticism. Coming together back at their Dinard base to watch England take on Iceland in their Round of 16 clash, Wales' Dragons celebrated feverishly as Iceland secured a fantastic 2–1 victory over Roy Hodgson's men – which wasn't as unexpected to myself and many others as the English press had uncharitably tended to make out. The Welsh boys went crazy in celebration, delirious at the fact that another team of underdogs (some of whom were teammates, remember) had succeeded in toppling the English. Don't get me wrong, I'm sure the fact that it was England who had been knocked out had some effect on the celebrations, but some branded it as unsporting and disrespectful... Many completely disagreed – not many English, mind, but one very famous one did. Alan Shearer had this to say on the subject: 'I don't see that being an issue at all – they've earned the right to celebrate, they've earned the right to be here. If I was a Wales player I wouldn't care whether that came out at all – they've been brilliant throughout this tournament so far and they're well within their right to enjoy it. England aren't in the quarter-finals – Wales are!' Yes, we were; and next Wales' Dragons had to avoid being slain by Marc Wilmots' Red Devils. Back to Lille then, for a game that would take Wales onto an entirely different level in every sense!

CHAPTER 7

Wales vs Belgium

Stade Pierre Mauroy, Lille – 1 July 2016

'If we ever beat that, if we ever get a better
performance than that, then it means we've
just won the World Cup.'

OWAIN TUDUR JONES,
FORMER WALES INTERNATIONAL

Journalist: Where do you get your motivation to play
every game at the highest level?

Gareth Bale: The dragon on my shirt, that's all I need.

CUE MASS EXPLOSION OF PRIDE IN WELSH HEARTS

NOT MONEY, NOT sponsorships, not the spotlight,
just the dragon on our shirt, on our flag – doing it
for Wales. Something we can all buy into, and boy
did we do that! An explosion is an understatement
– I think everyone just went absolutely insane for
that answer. As Andrew Gwilym said previously,
you get a lot of bluster from footballers these days
in press conferences, but this was just so genuine, so
perfect an answer. That sentence characterised Wales'

entire tournament – these guys weren't fighting for material gain, they weren't fighting for themselves as individuals; they were fighting for each other, for Wales, to put our wonderful little nation on the map. Our heroes were putting in a seismic performance that was forcing an entire continent to sit up and take notice of the raucous sporting revolution that was taking place in our country. After decades of skirting around the edges of the action, Wales had well and truly barnstormed its way back onto the international stage.

That comment from Bale was where this match kicked off, really. Two days before the game, everyone had just about taken on board the momentous events of the previous couple of weeks, and started looking ahead to this. All of us as Wales fans, particularly the younger generations, have heard our friends or elders talking about '76 or '58 and what it was like to see Wales contesting the quarter-finals of a major tournament, but this was a moment for all generations to enjoy. We all thought we understood it and that we knew how we'd feel if we were ever lucky enough to see the same thing. I certainly did: I thought I had it sussed and that I'd take it in my stride, but boy, was I wrong! As far as I was concerned, hearing Bale say those words was as good as winning the tournament. Look at the other tournament superstars, were any of them putting out statements like that to world? It's a sentiment we've all echoed about Bale and his fantastically proud, talented teammates over the years, but hearing those words come out of his mouth, you just think, 'Thank God this guy is one of ours. Thank God he feels this way about Wales and that each and every one of them in that squad feels the same. Thank God Chris Coleman, Osian Roberts, Ryland Morgans, Ian Mitchell et al. work their arses off for our team. Thank God Wales got it right' – and we haven't even got to the game yet!

Dylan Ebenezer was one of the lucky few to be sitting in Wales' Dinard media centre when Bale spoke those words, and he recalled the moment vividly: 'I was lucky enough to be sat there when the Belgian reporter asked Bale what motivates him to play for Wales, and he had that little grin on his face again and he said 'The dragon on my shirt, that's all I need.' ... you could just hear the gasp going around the press room as all of the journalists were thinking 'Thank you!' and just got their heads down and started typing stories about what was a dream of a quote! He means every word of it though – that quote was so ridiculous and everyone just loved it. It was turning into the Gareth Bale show in press conferences, fair play, but he is one hell of a guy so why not? Gunter, Taylor, Davies, Allen, Ramsey, Robson-Kanu, King, Vokes, Bale – they were all brilliant in their press conferences! Their manner was inspiring – the journalists were all inspired by it, so I can't imagine what it does for the team!' From #TogetherStronger to #TheDragonOnMyShirt, those comments sparked a new craze for Welsh football fans. The phones and devices of the likes of Rob Dowling, who is responsible for the FAW Twitter feed, were running out of battery simply because of the number of interactions they were getting on social media, as thousands of ardent fans showed hundreds of thousands of followers how proud they were to be wearing that beautiful red jersey.

This was the pinnacle of our tournament, without a doubt, but it didn't feel like it was going to end in Lille. Something about Belgium has always seemed to bring the best out in us, one way or another, and their FA representative's admission after the draw for the group stages – noted earlier – that they were relieved not to have drawn Wales in their group said that Wales would have a psychological edge if nothing else, if the Dragons could stamp their authority on the game early on.

The fans certainly stamped their authority on the city, despite being hopelessly outnumbered by the Belgians. The whole group was in Lille the day before Wales faced off with England, and we did a good job of filling the city, but with the Belgians there it was absolutely rammed! A total takeover: football fans were just everywhere – mostly Belgians, because of the proximity to the border, no doubt – with Lille just about brought to a standstill as a result. Again, everyone congregated outside Lille Flandres station, and the Belgians were fantastic fans – confident, incredibly jolly, good sports – but there were at least twice as many fans there as had been there for our last visit to Lille. The fountain outside the station was full of inflatable objects: sheep, dragons, sticks, thumbs, boats, bubble bath even – the lot! Flares were going off, plastic cups carpeted the floor, everyone was singing and dancing together, taking selfies, hugging, wishing each other a good hiding with the biggest of grins on our faces – this was just it. We'd all been saying it couldn't get better, game after game after game, but it really felt like it was never going to get better than this.

On the tram, snaking its way through the suburbs of Lille on the way to the stadium, I really got a sense of just how outnumbered our fans were on the day. Travelling to Lille on my own for this one had seemed like a great idea, but then to be heading towards the stadium with only two other Welsh fans in a ten-car tram full of Belgians over two hours before the game, you start to think 'uh-oh'... Not because you're in danger or anything – they were fantastic fans – but we were just so outnumbered it was unbelievable. They absolutely deafened us, singing their songs about Eden Hazard, Kevin De Bruyne and some of their players from the nineties who were pretty useful. To be fair, they did give us three – total strangers to each other who had congregated together on the tram all thinking the same thing – the chance to do our best to belt the anthem out, and we did so, arm-in-arm... Football, eh? That's why we love it! Despite the language barrier, the Belgians were gesturing to the three of us about what their guys had done to Hungary in their previous game – securing a 4–0 win in the last 16 – and how they were going to do the same to Wales in this one... we'd soon see!

The £200m. Stade Pierre-Mauroy, which had only opened four years previously, was mostly filled with Belgians, with the Welsh given what felt like an away allocation for yet another game, but it mattered little as we were all just immensely happy to be there and the whole occasion was just perfect. Torrential rain did its best to douse our enthusiasm, but the Welsh could have been hit by a tsunami and it would have had little effect. Lille's stadium had a retractable roof, which many had hoped would be closed, but given how dry the pitches had been in previous Wales games, it was something of a blessing in disguise that the pitch had been watered one way or another before this monumental clash. Everything just seemed to be falling right for us! No more so than with the line-ups, because although Belgium had romped home against Hungary, there were a few things that needed to be considered.

Firstly, Hungary had sort of played into the hands of Marc Wilmots' side towards the end of the game, losing their defensive discipline in trying to go toe-to-toe with the Red Devils in search of an equaliser, having been 1–0 down since the tenth minute. When you're facing Hazard, De Bruyne and co., nine times out of ten you're going to be picked off if you do that. Wales fielded a team of players who were very experienced against Belgium, and wouldn't repeat those mistakes, but certainly the fact Belgium had destroyed Hungary helped Wales build up their much-loved underdog mentality again. On top of that, Thomas Vermaelen had been booked for the second time in the tournament during that Toulouse clash, meaning he would miss the game against Wales. He had arguably been Wilmots' most important player up to that point as well, with Vincent Kompany missing the tournament through injury. Jan Vertonghen would also miss out, after picking up an injury in the build-up to this quarter-final clash in Lille.

This meant that Belgium would line up with a back four of Thomas Meunier, Jason Denayer, Toby Alderweireld and Jordan Lukaku – Alderweireld aside, that defence had a combined 20 caps between them. Not only that, but they were all very young players, averaging 22 years of age. Now, you might point to James Chester and say he only had 15 Wales caps at that point, which is obviously true, but he was 27 years old, and had made something like 200+ career appearances, playing in a wealth of different situations and systems. Just seeing their back four seemed to boost Welsh confidence, because most people had never heard of the full backs, and what they remembered of Denayer and Alderweireld was how they were given a really rough night by Hal Robson-Kanu and co. just over a year previously.

Ashley Williams had come out of the Northern Ireland game in a sling, with numerous questions marks throughout the period between that match and the quarter-final clash over his likelihood of starting against Belgium. A number of journalists noted a particular reluctance from Williams to move his left arm when needing to do things like scratch his face or move his microphone in his pre-match press conference, despite prior confirmation from the FAW that Williams would play. Maybe we were all just over-analysing things – the pessimism coming out again and whatnot – but as James Chester remarked, none of those players were going to miss that game unless they only had one leg to stand on, and even then they'd have done everything in their power to take part!

Talking of legs, Joe Ledley was still going strong too, which was incredible considering the workload he'd put his recently fractured fibula through over the last few weeks, featuring in four games in two weeks. This meant that Wales were able to field their go-to team against Belgium, but despite this there were still some niggling doubts in the back of everyone's minds. Many people were confident we'd win if we played to our potential – in fact, I think everyone was – but we just couldn't get over the fact that this was happening to us! We were in a quarter-final, against a team who hated playing us and were somewhat under strength, and we had a shot at making the semi-finals of our first ever Euros... The whole tournament was an experience that left you shaking your head with disbelief, but with the opportunity presented to us here, some fans didn't dare to believe we could do it. It just seemed too amazingly good to be true that we were on this stage with this opportunity!

Owain Tudur Jones, again working for S4C on another fantastic night for Welsh football, said that this was the first time he felt the unease that some of the players had admitted to feeling against Northern Ireland in the previous game. 'That's the one – the one that'll live long in the memory for so many reasons. Maybe the Russia game was all about free-flowing football because of the space we were provided with, but this game had everything. This was the first time I felt strange about the fact that we could be going home. I was standing outside the stadium doing a live interview for S4C; it was raining quite badly. All of a sudden we saw a helicopter, which we soon realised was following the Belgium team coach, then that came into the stadium and the players came out etc. Next thing there's another helicopter and it's Wales this time. We saw that one come in – that's when I had that weird feeling. These two coaches were coming into the ground for the game, and afterwards one of them was going home – I don't know, something just hit me then, that this was proper knockout football. I know we'd had a knockout game against Northern

Ireland too, but this was the first time I properly felt it.'

The enormity of the occasion was certainly felt by all. It was quite strange because the walkways down to the seating areas were just enormous and begging to be filled with celebrating fans, but even before the match there were fans sitting on those walkway steps with their heads in their hands, just in bits thinking about the amazing journey Wales had been on up to this point. Normally you see that after a game, where your team has been relegated or something like that – we've all seen it on TV or unfortunately experienced it ourselves – but there were just a few people sitting in the walkways in tears because of Bordeaux, Lens, Toulouse, Paris and now Lille. It had all come down to this moment. We'd all had the time of our lives, an experience that I imagine (and was told by people who'd been through such things themselves) is only topped by getting married or seeing your new-born child for the first time. That's the context of what Wales had achieved, and everybody was just drunk on that feeling of delirium, the emotion of being on a stage that they never wanted to have to step down from and leave behind.

Then kick-off came and – as the first country ever to sing their national anthem before a sporting event, starting the trend in 1905 at a Welsh rugby match – if this was the last time we were ever going to sing it at a major tournament, or at least for another few years, then we were going to make absolutely sure that it was heard loud and clear. Outnumbered five to one in the stadium, we still sang our anthem as loud as – if not louder than – the Belgians sang theirs. Unfortunately that was the last time Wales' Dragons were equal to the Red Devils... for the next ten minutes or so, anyway. Wilmots' men came tearing out of the blocks in what was pretty much a carbon copy of the opening exchanges of the two sides' previous clash in Cardiff, except the Belgians this time appeared to have more of a cutting edge about them. Yannick Carrasco and Hazard started on the flanks in a 4–3–3 formation, with Romelu Lukaku leading the line, De Bruyne, Radja Nainggolan and Axel Witsel in midfield, and the young full backs Meunier and the younger Lukaku bombing forward. Wales took punch after punch after punch. It was just an unyielding attacking performance from the then-second-best team in the world, and things looked pretty bleak. It turned out to be an absolutely pulsating, unbelievable thriller of a game, worthy of the tournament final.

Ben Davies was booked after five minutes, incredibly harshly, after giving away the game's first foul. This landed him with a suspension for any potential semi-final berth, but that wasn't to be the last of Wales' problems in the opening exchanges. Kevin De Bruyne advanced through the middle two minutes later on a counter-attack, with Davies – moments after receiving a booking for fouling the same player –

understandably somewhat hesitant to stick a foot in, and the Manchester City playmaker was able to offload the ball to Romelu Lukaku on the left. He floated the ball in towards the far post, where Carrasco was unmarked to shoot, but Hennessey blocked... into the path of Meunier, whose shot was blocked, this time by Neil Taylor... into the path of Hazard, who shot over from the edge of the area. Wales were still alive, just, after a breathless start to the match. All the singing in the world from the Welsh fans wasn't affecting the Belgians – they weren't intimidated at that point, they were out for blood, desperate to go ahead and take control of the game early on.

When the goal did come, you couldn't say Belgium were undeserving of it after 12 minutes of destructive dominance that seemed to leave Wales' dreams of reaching the semi-finals in tatters. Nainggolan had the ball laid off to him by Hazard a good 30 yards away from goal, where he found himself totally unmarked and rifled a first-time effort beyond Hennessey into the top corner for the lead. A stunning, hammer-blow of a goal, worthy of putting a team into the lead so early on in the quarter-finals. What happened next was unbelievable. Joe Ledley was brutally honest in his summation of the opening exchanges: 'I remember thinking the first five or ten minutes were the worst we'd ever come across – we weren't great, they had a few chances – but once they scored they just sort of dropped in and tried to hang on to the lead, which was a bit strange. Then once we got the ball, we relaxed, we outplayed them and outclassed them in every area from that point onwards!'

I think Joe's being a bit modest there personally, because it sounds like he's saying Belgium just dropped in and waited to counter – that's not how I saw it at all. Once they went behind, Wales kicked the game off again and completely drained the Belgians of any momentum they'd gained by going ahead. Wales kept the ball, moved it quickly, didn't let Belgium sit still – if they wanted that ball back, they were going to have to chase it. If there's one criticism you can level at the Belgians, it's that they don't seem to fight – they don't seem to have that spirit to keep going, to keep chasing, to keep plugging away. That's when they dropped in, because they didn't have it in them to out-battle Wales. It's not that they chose to: their lack of desire and spirit left them with no other choice than to do that, and Wales duly snatched the initiative of the game from Marc Wilmots' men.

Andrew Gwilym concurred, contrasting Wales' fightback in the Belgium clash with the lack of fight shown by England in their last-16 defeat to Iceland. 'You look how England reacted to going behind against the minnows of the tournament, and how Wales responded to going a goal down against one of the favourites... I thought it summed the difference between the two sides up completely, in terms of spirit and ability to handle pressure. England went totally into their shells and rarely looked like scoring at any point after that, whereas Wales, for the 15 minutes after Nainggolan scored that goal, had 65% of the possession. They totally dominated the ball, and if you've just scored and you've had a good start, you desperately want another one, don't you? You're buzzing, you're confident – but Wales took that away from them and totally sapped their energy in that 15-minute period. People like Hazard, Lukaku and Carrasco had to start dropping in because they couldn't get the ball... We wiped out all of their momentum.'

What more is there to say about Wales' initial response? 65% possession against Belgium, after going 1–0 down. Much as the 3–5–2 had worked perfectly for Wales against Bosnia – and other teams – way back in qualifying, it did so here too, because Wales' three centre backs occupied Belgium's three forwards. The question then was, what do you do with Taylor and Gunter? Push them forward and go for it, risking a 3v3 if you're countered, or sit back and wait for a counter-attack of your own? Wales had no choice: they went for it. Interestingly, though – probably because of their makeshift defence – Belgium didn't want to expose any defensive problems and, as a result, Hazard and Carrasco dropped off a bit, instead of pushing up, leaving Lukaku to fend for himself against three defenders. Wales' wing backs, meanwhile, pushed up and Belgium's wingers weren't very disciplined in tracking them, leaving Jordan Lukaku and Meunier exposed. They had to push up to meet Wales' Gunter and Taylor when running forward, leaving space in behind which Wales exploited brilliantly. We pinpointed Hazard in *The Dragon Roars Again* as a bit of a problem for Belgium when they play Wales, mainly in an attacking sense and in not being able to combine well with De Bruyne, but in this game it was his and Carrasco's lack of defensive work that caused Belgium problems.

Neil Taylor, having got off the mark for Wales with that goal against Akinfeev in the final group game, went agonisingly close to scoring his second of the tournament to equalise. Ramsey danced into the box, got to the byline and cut the ball back into the empty space by the penalty spot which Taylor was running into. He side-footed a driven effort low and hard towards goal – how Courtois saved it, I don't think any of us knew, but it was such an enormous opportunity, exceptionally saved... You just end up thinking, 'What if that was THE chance to draw us level?' But it wasn't. Wales kept on making life hell for the Belgians, and soon had their equaliser thanks to another unlikely source, with an hour left on the clock. Robson-Kanu, yet again making an absolute nuisance of himself, won a corner for Wales, which Ramsey swung in towards the criminally unmarked Ashley Williams. He left Courtois no chance with his header – the ball nestling just inside the near post which De Bruyne had abandoned – and Wales were back on level terms! I'd love to be able to put into words what that noise was like as everyone celebrated – how biblical it was, how relentless – but I think the best word to describe what we all felt is relief. We were all screaming our heads off, gripping each other, jumping on each other's backs – just absolutely losing every bit of sense we had in celebration. We'd all said we'd win if we played to our potential, and here we were, back in the game against one of the best teams in the world and we didn't look like stopping there. Never mind the prospect of beating Belgium, Wales could have beaten any team in the world the way they played after going behind.

This wasn't backs against the wall any more, like we'd been used to when Wales played Belgium. This time our Dragons had the Red Devils exactly where they wanted them and knew it, which showed exactly how far this amazing team had come. As Ian Gwyn Hughes noted, 'I think the last few games against Belgium – winning 1–0, drawing 0–0 and drawing 1–1 – there have been elements of backs against the wall in the performances. Then you have three attempts cleared off the line in Lille, they score a fantastic goal and you're thinking we could get hammered here. After that, Marc Wilmots said in his press conference after the match that he couldn't understand what happened, whether Belgium just thought it would be easy or what, but once we equalised I think we put the seeds of doubt in their minds. They had a couple of good chances, but we weren't going into the unknown – we knew them, we'd played them recently, and it must have been in the back of their minds – the past results we'd got against them. Doesn't that show how much this team has developed though?' Even the day before the game, the Belgian FA representatives had told the FAW they couldn't believe these two teams had been drawn to play each other again, so there was obviously something in it: that they just didn't want to play Wales.

Now Chris Coleman's men were well and truly back in the game and, going into half-time, it looked like there'd only be one winner when the teams came back out for the second half. 'I don't think anyone could say anything at half-time, just more of the same, and we did that – we kept our shape and broke with pace,' Joe Ledley said. 'When they do break, they break in numbers and they're easy to counter-attack because they don't get back into shape as well as we do – you could see that in the game. Once we'd survived the brunt of their attack it was easy for us to get the ball down, find our two 10s in Bale and Rambo, and take it from there. We couldn't just sit back and let them come at us. We wanted to put them on the back foot, and we did it with every opportunity we had.'

Belgium started the second half in the way they began the first: throwing everything at the Wales goal, with Hazard and Lukaku both wasting chances. Again, after surviving the opening ten minutes of the half, Wales went back on the offensive and provided Europe with a goal that will be watched and practised and wept over again and again and again, not just by the Welsh but by anyone who loves the beautiful game. Hal Robson-Kanu would continue his incredible run of scoring winning goals for Wales – four goals, four match-winners – but this one was by far the most important, the most amazing, the most tear-jerking. It just had everything! Bale, Ramsey and Robson-Kanu have combined one way or another for numerous important goals for Wales over the last few years, but none of them have ever come close to this.

Bale picked the ball up from Gunter inside his own half, jogged down the right wing under no pressure and found Ramsey, who was making a great run across the defence to the right-hand side of the box, with a great lofted pass. Ramsey, who was superb all night (despite being very harshly booked), – all tournament in fact – had a fantastic touch, picking out Robson-Kanu, surrounded by three defenders in the box. Everyone was screaming for HRK to leave the ball to run on for Taylor, who was arriving unmarked on the far side of the box, but he didn't. He came, he Cruyff-turned, Wales conquered – to paraphrase Julius Caesar rather poorly! Three defenders left for dead as Robson-Kanu Cruyff-turned on the spot, in traffic, selling the defenders with a move to find himself one-on-one with Courtois, then slotting home from seven yards out to put Wales 2–1 up on the night!

'This is unbelievable, what a run from Ramsey – Fellaini doesn't track him. He gets in behind then plays the ball in to Robson-Kanu: just watch this for a Cruyff turn. If that was Messi, they'd be talking about it for years... just watch this! See you later, Meunier! See you later, Denayer! See you later, Fellaini! He had the composure to open his body up and stick it past Courtois – 2–1 Wales, great team!' Or, as Robbie Savage would also say later on in the night – slightly more intoxicated than when he had said those words in the commentary, 'He sent three Belgium players – one went for a coffee, one went for a tea, one went for a pie – if Messi does a trick like that the world talks about it for years. Robson-Kanu is a free agent, he hasn't got a club, scored three goals in the Championship last season and has put defenders to shame! Wales! They could win it!'

Even writing those words now, I well up a little bit, thinking about that goal. The excitement of the ball being at Bale's feet, Ramsey making a great run, wondering if they'll find each other. The awe at Ramsey's touch, the fact that he's able to get the ball into the box. The frustration that the ball isn't left for Taylor – suddenly thinking he's become Robert Lewandowski because he scored one goal against Russia, and that he's surely in a better position than Hal. This all followed by the sheer disbelief and feeling of time standing still as HRK, or Hal Johan-Kanu as we should all now call him, made that turn, and the sound as everyone pretty much lost their minds thinking we'd just gone ahead, before the ball had even gone in, then the delirium as we all realised what we, little old Wales, were 35 minutes away from achieving. A group of grown men next to me were having a pile-on on the floor, all laughing, screaming, crying, just hysterical at what was going on. Those massive walkways were crammed with fans, the most enormous, jubilant mosh-pit of celebrating football fans in history, and there we were: beating Belgium again, so close to unthinkable glory!

Time wore on. Belgium kept trying, but they were constantly shut out by a fiercely determined Wales, with the Dragons clinging onto that lead until we were into the last five minutes. The tension was almost suffocating, but physio Sean Connelly popping Neil Taylor in the head drastically changed the mood amongst the bench and the guys on the pitch, as the wing back recalled. 'I went to get a drink from the touchline and they threw me a bottle of water, and I threw it back because I needed something with flavour or something to help me with cramp... They threw me one of them instead and Sean tried to throw a gel onto the pitch for Aaron, but he hit me on the head with it somehow from about 30 feet away. I was shouting at him, everyone else was laughing at me and it just relieved the tension really, because otherwise they'd have all been stressing about subs, who was marking who on corners – everything – and

I think Sean just pelting me in the head with that gel snapped everyone out of it... Everyone was laughing, even the manager!'

At that point, it's a case of kick it to the corner, keep it there and run down the clock – maybe a bit early for that mentality, but we all wanted our team to cling onto the lead, so why not do everything to secure it? Even the bench was of that opinion as, with five minutes to go, Chris Gunter again advanced down the right-hand side with the players on the bench screaming for him to keep the ball in the corner and let time slip away for the Belgians. He had other ideas. With substitute Sam Vokes storming into the area, running across the face of the six-yard box towards the near post, Dries Mertens gave Gunter just enough space to get a cross into the box, and Vokes – fittingly nicknamed Tosh by his fellow teammates – glanced it in emphatically before storming off to the corner to celebrate, an expression on his face so full of joy and incredulity that he looked somewhat possessed.

'There were so many Belgians in there, it was almost like an away game – being so close to Belgium, they obviously fancied the match and made the trip,' Vokes said. 'As the match went on, though, you couldn't hear the Belgians – just the Welsh fans, constantly singing. That sea of red in the corner – it was absolutely unbelievable. I can't describe that feeling when I scored the third goal, not even if I tried. I felt like a fan at that point. When the ball hit the back of the net we all just ran to the corner flag and went nuts with the fans right next to us – such a good feeling.' James Chester, like the rest of us probably, chose that moment – knowing we were going to beat Belgium, having performed the way we had just done – as his standout memory in football. 'On that stage, having gone a goal behind and having to fight our way back into the game, playing ourselves back in front, withstanding a bit of pressure... once that goal had gone in, with the time that was left in the game, I just knew we'd won and done enough to get into the semi-finals, achieving something that no-one imagined we could do. To achieve that with the group of lads we've got, the staff, the coaching staff and the fans there with us too, I think that is probably the best moment I've had on a football pitch in my career.'

I'd like to say things changed after that final goal, that we sang louder, that we threw further support behind the boys, but we didn't – we couldn't have. We'd given them everything since the first minute, silencing the Belgians, who vastly outnumbered us, and we were rewarded a million times over by our Dragons that night in Lille. That goal and the two preceding it sent 10,000 Welsh fans on their way to the promised land, as they realised they were witnessing history, in the presence of the first Welsh team ever to reach the semi-finals of a major tournament! Missing out in 1958 and 1976, 2016 was the year the unthinkable happened. Third time lucky and all that; but the team being 'lucky' doesn't even come into the equation when considering what the Welsh faithful witnessed as the Dragons completed their most historic victory on that amazing July night. Sure, those 10,000 fans were exceptionally lucky to have seats inside the stadium to witness history being made, but there was nothing lucky about Wales' decimation of Belgium – Chris Coleman's men absolutely eviscerated the opposition on the way to booking an unbelievable semi-final berth for Euro 2016.

The celebrations after the full-time whistle were amazing. The players mimicked their running towards us and diving along the grass after the qualification party against Andorra nine months earlier; Joe Ledley danced; we all sang the anthem over and over again; the Icelandic clap was given a run-out – it was just a symphony of perfection, something very few of us had ever dreamed we'd witness. Wales in the European Championship semi-finals... what had we done!? I can't put into words what it meant for everyone to be there and witness Wales achieve that, but here are some insights from a few men who are far better qualified than me to speak about the significance of Wales' achievements in Lille that night:

Jonny Williams: Celebrating in front of the fans after that game is one of the moments we'll probably never get again. We created history together. Personally, after all the ups and downs of my short career so far, it was just something I had to stand there and take in for a minute. I was just looking around thinking, 'What am I doing here?' You know? Myself, Ben and Wardy came through together and there we all were, celebrating that, and we all knew how special and incredible it was. We were on social media afterwards and noticed how the team huddle evolved into a heart shape – we just thought it was meant to be from then.

Jack Collison: What a performance, and the goals were amazing! Hal Robson-Kanu – man, I think that goal is going to be shown on screens for many years to come. There will be kids re-enacting that in their gardens for just as long, too. I think that was why this tournament became such a big success for Wales. They've been together for so long and they've chipped away at things to try and make this work – losing 6–1 to Serbia a few years ago, remember – and now they've got to this tournament and they've created some of the biggest highs they're ever going to experience, on an enormous stage in front of some of the craziest fans in the world. It was brilliant!

Rob Dowling: After the Belgium game a Czech Republic commentator came over to me and asked if I was with the Wales team. I said yes, and he told me this was the most special moment of his 28 years in the business, seeing what Wales were doing at that tournament. I couldn't respond, I just had to give him a hug and shed a few tears. It shows how far what we did at the tournament has resonated with everyone else... I think we've been genuine in every sense, which must be refreshing for the established nations – the likes of us and Iceland just came there to play football and enjoy the experience.

Raymond Verheijen: Without a doubt, I'm so proud of the guys. I was already proud of them before the tournament because, given what's happened, they stuck together very strongly and, by qualifying for the first time, they would have made Gary extremely proud! Reaching the semi-finals is even more incredible. Even though it was nearly five years ago, I think it's fair to say that Gary Speed was the father of this success, by changing the culture of Welsh football and building this team. But Chris Coleman has done an incredible job to continue that process, doing it his way, and he deserves massive credit for that. I'm very proud of each and every one of them for what they've achieved, and Gary would be too!

James Chester: That game was almost two years after I made my debut for Wales against Holland, and I'd be lying if I told you I expected then to be on that stage against Belgium in two years' time. When I spoke to the gaffer about coming to play for Wales, it was a great opportunity in my mind to go and test myself at another level, against some of the best strikers and players that Europe had to offer at an international level, and see if I could improve myself from there. Meeting up for the first time against Holland, in those meetings everyone was talking about how confident we were of getting to the Euros, but I don't think any of us in our wildest dreams imagined getting to anything like that stage against Belgium, and then going one step further still!

Owain Tudur Jones: If we ever beat that, if we ever get a better performance than that, then it means we've just won the World Cup.

That quote from OTJ summed the night up perfectly – if we ever have a more glorious night than that, with a better performance, it'll have to be winning the greatest, most prestigious tournament in football. Welsh fans were treated to a guard of honour by their Belgian counterparts as they returned to Lille city centre after the game – top class fans, they really were, shaking every Welsh fan's hand, congratulating us and wishing us well for the next round. Funnily enough, on the way back, I spotted the same fans I'd met on the tram on the way to the game and we shook hands as they shook their heads in disbelief – frankly we were having trouble believing this amazing night in Lille had happened too! But there was another game to come – roll on Lyon, where Portugal awaited Wales' delirious Dragons!

CHAPTER 8

Portugal vs Wales

Stade de Lyon – 6 July 2016

'It's too big an opportunity, too huge a legacy
to let slip through your fingers! Football in Wales
could be redefined on the back of what's happened
in France, and I hope it is.'

ANDREW GWILYM, WELSH FOOTBALL JOURNALIST.

'DON'T TAKE ME HOME! PLEASE, DON'T TAKE
ME HOME! I JUST DON'T WANT TO GO TO WORK!'
Forget anything you'll find in the iTunes charts –
apart from The Barry Horns, the Super Furries or the
Manics of course – this was the anthem of the summer!
Bouncing up and down in a heart-shaped huddle near
a corner flag in Lille, Wales' heroes were having the
time of their lives in front of the best supporters in
the world; some of whom – never mind not wanting
to go to work – had quit their jobs on the back of the
Dragons' success in France in the summer of 2016.
Quitting jobs, cancelling holidays, upsetting partners,
not seeing their kids for a few more days... whatever
people had to do to follow Wales on this journey, they

did it, no matter how difficult it was, and every second of it was absolutely bloody glorious.

Gianluca Vialli had it spot on when he spoke on the BBC after Wales' victory over Belgium in Lille, and his words were as descriptive of the fans' immense commitment as they were of the players' achievements. 'I was so inspired last night. Their spirit was amazing, and with organisation and spirit you can climb mountains and make miracles. They have respect, but no fear. It's the season of the underdogs: Leicester, Wales, maybe Italy!' An article on *Wales Online*, written by the excellent Chris Wathan, spoke of the 11 defining moments from Wales' historic victory over Belgium in Lille – I'm sure Chris could have come up with 1,100 if he'd been given the word count. It was just one of those amazing days from start to finish.

After such an incredible experience, even though there's another game to come, you can't help but feel somewhat relaxed, like this is the pinnacle. 'It was sort of like we were on a stag do really; obviously without the drinking and so on, but we were having the time of our lives,' Joe Ledley said of the entire Euro 2016 experience. 'We didn't want to be going home, having people asking us what the Euros were like and we just answer 'Oh, it was OK – it was a bit long,' you know? We wanted to enjoy it! You want to tell people it was the best time of your life, and that's what it was – we made every moment special, together as a team, and we enjoyed it. That's what you need to do! There's no point finishing your career and saying we should have done more as a team or should have bonded more – we'd done exactly that since day one, and for me it was fantastic. It'll stay with me forever. I could name 50 standout memories, maybe more – every day was a pleasure to work with those guys and the staff. It was just a fantastic journey and I loved every single minute of it.'

If this was to be journey's end in Lyon, what a beautiful place for it to happen. Most of the cities that hosted Wales throughout this tournament could be accused of treating Welsh fans to pretty rubbish weather – usually right up until the game came around, rather fittingly. Only in Lille was there bad weather for the actual match, against Belgium, and, let's be honest, nobody gave a damn that night! Lyon was what France in the summer should have been like – 30+ degrees, barely a cloud in the sky – and full of Welsh fans who had no suncream with them and were just looking for shade... especially me, with my ginger hair! I don't think any of us will have ever seen a sky like it. It was just beautiful: perfect, sapphire blue, and with the sun beaming out it felt like nothing could go wrong, not even when it came to the game. Again though, the expectations seemed to go through the roof. You could hardly blame people after the euphoria of Lille, but I guess as Wales fans, in a weird way, we're more comfortable when we're worried about the game ahead, not confident.

On the TGV down to Lyon from Paris, I met an incredible gentleman who was in Sweden – no, not at the 3–0 defeat a few weeks earlier, but in 1958 when Wales lost to Brazil in the World Cup quarter-finals. You just can't comprehend what it means to be that man. Listening to the stories of what he had witnessed – I didn't even get his name, but there should be statues of people like him outside Welsh stadiums in years to come as much as there should be one of Gareth Bale or whoever, because of what he'd been through, what he'd seen and where; just that undying love and desire to follow Welsh football for an entire lifetime. It's no secret that we all got emotional at one point or another – at every opportunity possible, for most us, no doubt – but seeing people like Gary Pritchard, Dylan Llewelyn, Rob Phillips and Chris Wathan, who had watched hundreds of Wales games over the course of their lives, just overjoyed and broken at the same time because of what they'd seen in France after the darker times they'd suffered following Wales, I think of the immense impact of this past summer on every type of Wales fan. From the well-known ones in the media to the elderly gentleman I met on the train – it touched everyone profoundly.

Chris and I actually bumped into each other at the station in Lille the morning after Belgium. Normally I don't know what to say because I'm in awe of people like him, Gary, Dylan, Rob – anyone like that – after what they've been through with Wales, but this time we just had a bit of a hug because we were both spent after an amazing night we never thought in our wildest dreams would have turned out the way that it did. We both knew we could beat Belgium, of course, but to do it like that... The emotion, the celebrations and the ecstasy of it exhausted everyone who was there to witness it, but we were getting to go again for Portugal and neither of us knew what to say about it... except 'see you there, pal!' because neither of us would have missed it for the world.

Chris Coleman's pre-tournament message to the fans was to go out to France and enjoy it; to soak every second of it up and love it, revel in it, cherish it – and we certainly did – and the team, he said, would do the same if they performed. If it had ever been in doubt before Wales' quarter-final against Belgium, there could be no doubt heading into Lyon for the Portugal game that the Dragons were performing to levels that even the most optimistic of Wales fans before the tournament would have struggled to predict. 'By the time we got to the quarter-finals and the semi-finals, we were the most relaxed team in the tournament by far,' the FAW's Mark Evans said. 'There was no fear whatsoever. Everyone was enjoying it and they went into every game with the right attitude. There was still the same intensity in the training sessions, but we were all so relaxed within ourselves by then because we'd shown we were a good team, we'd shown what we were capable of. Gareth Bale was having selfies with all of the people working in the stadium without them even asking him to – it was that kind of attitude really, where we were just happy to be there and playing to our best potential.'

Taking part in BBC Radio Cymru's *Ar Y Marc* in the build-up to the semi-final were some contributors and supporters who were saying this was a game too far for Wales, but also there were those who were saying that Portugal had ridden their luck massively to get to this point. They had scraped through their group in third place and had then gone on to need at least extra time in each of their knockout games, a far cry from the flamboyant Latin style we were all used to seeing from Ronaldo and his teammates. They'd beaten Croatia and Poland though, who were two dark horses tipped to go far in the tournament, so who was to say they couldn't do the same to Wales? Having said that, Pepe – arguably their player of the tournament up this point – was out injured, so there were definitely positives to take into the game for Wales.

'We watched them and thought, given that they'd been to extra time in every knockout game they'd played, they had to be tired, they had to be struggling… and Pepe was out injured, so we thought we had a good chance,' Neil Taylor said of Wales' initial expectations of their semi-final opponents. 'Once we watched them, though – after Belgium we sat down and watched what they'd done in their quarter-final – we quickly realised that they were probably the best defensive team in the tournament. At least since they'd got out of the group, they'd been very, very good. They played quite direct to Ronaldo whenever they had the ball, he'd put it out wide then make his way into the box to try and get his head on a cross – but it was a very different style to what you'd expect from a Portugal or a Spain.'

After five games, we'd all picked up our habits and routines that we'd carry out before a game. For me, it was to wear the same clothes, because I'd worn a different top for England and we lost. My friend Gary Pritchard wore the same pair of yellow Wales socks for every game but the England match – allegedly washing them in between – and even FAW employees were taken by superstition. 'We all got quite superstitious, because we just noticed little things that we were doing every single time, yet for Portugal we couldn't follow them through. When we arrived at the stadium, we'd normally have an hour at the desk doing social media engagement, but the wifi wouldn't work for us – just us too, everyone else got on it without issue. We were late putting the teams out – I had to do updates from my phone for a time – so you just had a feeling that things weren't going to go to plan,' Rob Dowling said of his superstition woes in Lyon. 'Superstition is synonymous with football. I had my lucky pants on in Bordeaux but in Lens they were no good, so I ditched all my old superstitions after that and picked up new ones from the Russia game onwards! We were doing Tai Chi most nights – the only night we missed out on doing it was before the England match, so we ended up doing it every night whether it embarrassed us, or people could see us, or not.'

Of course, reaching the semi-finals has its perks for everyone involved. Firstly the occasion: I mean, come on, Wales in a semi-final... wow! Most of us were already black and blue from the raucous celebrations of the previous three weeks, but in this case any new bruises were because we were all pinching ourselves at the thought of us being where we were! Then there's the venue itself – if Toulouse's stadium was France's answer to the Old Wembley Stadium, the Stade de Lyon was France's answer to the new one... right down to the delays in getting the thing built! Up on a hill, state of the art – everything about it was befitting of a semi-final venue, but the facilities weren't most pleasing to everyone: 'What we had was the best studio that we'd had all tournament – it was a proper one, whereas the others were purpose-built for us,' said Owain Tudur Jones, who was working for S4C covering the match. 'This one was built into the stadium, like a Sky box that you're used to seeing on TV, but what that meant was that the glass was probably about six inches thick. We just couldn't get a feel of the atmosphere from in there, neither could we get out for the national anthem – although I did go for a look, I did ask people if there was anywhere we could go. It just didn't feel like we were living in the atmosphere of the game as it had done for the others.'

Two Welsh players in particular were forced to live in a different atmosphere to what they had been used to so far in the tournament too, as Ben Davies and Aaron Ramsey were both suspended for the semi-final – a major loss to the team. Davies talked about his conflicting feelings towards his suspension: 'Of course it was disappointing to get booked so early, but if it was to happen, I would have preferred it to happen then than towards the end of the game after knowing it was won. These things happen in football, and it's about dealing with them. I just told myself that I would do everything I could to get the boys to the semi-finals, which I helped them do. It was a horrible feeling sat in the stand against Portugal. I think I was more nervous having to do that than if I was playing – knowing that I could have no influence on the outcome of the game was hard.'

Dealing with what we were going through, in the same way that Ben had to deal with his suspension, was exhausting in some respects. When you win a quarter-final like Wales did against Belgium – dealing with all of the physical and mental exhaustion that comes with it for both players and fans – and when you're going on to face such a great side as Portugal, then you've got to keep everyone's feet on the ground.

Again, it's that expectation that just unsettles the whole team. You don't want it to infect the players – which it generally doesn't – nor the fans, because as soon as they have expectations, if things don't go the way they're expected to then it filters down to the pitch, just as it did against Northern Ireland.

The Dragons absolutely dominated the game against a top class side like Belgium, but on the other hand, Wales then have to go into a game with the double-whammy of missing Ramsey and Davies, so that brings expectations back down to earth a little bit and helps everyone, because then no one feels like Wales are at full strength and it brings the underdog mentality out again. Pepe – who was leading the tournament in terms of blocks, interceptions and clearances at the time – and William Carvalho being ruled out of the game for Portugal sort of swung the pendulum back Wales' way a bit, but whatever happened we just had to go and enjoy it. A lot of people dream about being on that stage – whether as a player or as a fan – but don't get the opportunity to fulfil it, so we all just had to remember that and revel in what would be the most unbelievable night of our lives (yes, we had a lot of them over the summer), regardless of the result.

Portugal had proved to be a very well-organised team, but few expected them to be a somewhat sterile side going forward in this match. We've all watched them for years and have become used to seeing them winning 4–3 or 3–2, playing flamboyant football with lots of tricks and fancy footwork. That sort of open game would have suited Wales on the night, but instead they were very organised, they had a good game plan and they stuck to it. They let Chris Coleman's men have the ball, dropped in and were really hard to break down. Although Cristiano Ronaldo is probably the first, second and third thing people think of when you mention Portugal's current football team, during Euro 2016 he hadn't even come close to being the 50-goal-a-season machine that has destroyed European defences for Real Madrid for the last seven years. Despite finding his scoring boots in a crucial last game of the group for Fernando Santos' men against Hungary, grabbing a brace in a 3–3 draw that saw Portugal through the group in third place, CR7 had taken on a very different role for Portugal in this tournament. He was definitely focusing on other parts of his game: becoming a team player, making countless defensive runs, constantly helping out his teammates and really stepping up in his role as captain.

A good example of this was in the penalty shoot-out against Poland, when Portugal were lacking a taker for the third penalty. João Moutinho didn't want to take one after missing in the shoot-out in the semi-final against Spain four years earlier, but Ronaldo managed to encourage his teammate to take the penalty. He also motivated the rest of the team throughout the entire shoot-out, giving them advice and support. Renato Sanches also had a great tournament for Portugal, and joined the likes of Nani and Ricardo Quaresma in taking the offensive load off Ronaldo by scoring the equaliser and winning Man of the Match against Poland (and becoming the third-youngest Euro scorer in history). However, even without Davies and Ramsey, Wales still had Portugal more or less contained in the first half.

Andy King missed a couple of half-chances for Wales in the opening 45 minutes, finding himself inches away from connecting with some dangerous crosses into the six-yard box, but otherwise Wales were significantly limited in their offensive play thanks to Portugal's stubborn set-up. Danilo Pereira was an absolute machine, cleaning up every single Wales attack as everything seemed to go exactly to plan for the Portuguese. 'Portugal were masters. They did what they did to Wales throughout the tournament – just look at how they knocked out Croatia. Croatia were sublime against them, but Portugal knocked them out because they had a game plan and they stuck to it,' Kit Symons said of Wales' dogged opponents, adamant that Portugal would be happy with their first-half performance. 'Portugal are just really, really good at stopping teams playing, and they did a job on us too – the first half was pretty boring, a poor 0–0, but they were happy because it probably went exactly how they'd planned it to go. I wasn't overly upset at half-time, because you're still 0–0 in a semi-final, but for them it must have gone exactly how they'd hoped.' What came next must have gone exactly how they'd hoped too, as Portugal had the game tied up eight minutes into the second half, thanks in no small part to that man, Cristiano Ronaldo. It was Sod's Law after a slow goal-scoring tournament that he'd turn the game on its head, but what a way to do it.

A delightful back-heeled goal against Austria in the group stages had shown the immense skill and finesse that CR7 is capable of, but for pure physical strength, athleticism and that scary movement and timing that you just can't teach, the Portuguese captain's goal to open the scoring against Wales was unbelievable. Well, for anyone except him – he always does this, and there's nothing anyone could do about it. To be fair though, it takes a lot to knock Wales out of tournaments. Pele in 1958, and Cristiano Ronaldo now landing a hammer blow to Wales' hopes after showing freakish power and poise from a corner, as Neil Taylor recalled. 'I remember seeing the ball going into the box, thinking it was going to fly out the other side without anyone getting anywhere near it, but then Ronaldo leaped. I've seen the clips back and James Chester got up there, he jumped really well, but Ronaldo was still a good couple of feet above him and you just can't compete with that. It wasn't like he wasn't marked, Chester was there, but once they got ahead you knew you weren't going to get many chances and it played into their hands then.'

Certainly the goal from the set piece showed why Ronaldo is probably one of the best to ever play the game. Not only is he brilliant technically, but physically he's an absolute freak! It's probably what's set him apart and made him as unbelievable as he has been throughout his career. This particular goal was a phenomenal effort and probably one that only he could have scored. You've got to feel sorry for James Chester really – he did bloody well both to stay with Ronaldo on the ground and also to leap ridiculously high in the air, only to be beaten by a guy who may as well be from another planet! He seems to have superpowers. That's what it looked like as he managed to jump a good two feet higher, on the way to powering a ridiculous header into the back of the net after 50 minutes. As against Belgium, what you want after that is time to get your feet back under the table and sap momentum from the opponents, but Ronaldo once again wouldn't have it. His shot from the edge of the box three minutes later rebounded hideously off Nani and into the back of the net, putting Portugal 2–0 up, and that was that.

Wales had run out of steam. With a game every few days for the past five weeks and the emotion of everything that had gone on beforehand in the tournament, the team was spent. Without Ramsey and Davies, Bale was resorting to dropping ridiculously deep to try and start plays and attempting potshots from 35–40 yards. Wales' journey in France had come to an end, but in the midst of all of this the fans were still going, still singing, still bouncing. Stinging a bit, undoubtedly, because we'd come so close to reaching the finals of the Euros at our first attempt, but by God what a journey we'd had as supporters – who'd have thought when we were in Bordeaux that we'd be here in Lyon, still going strong after three-and-a-bit weeks, singing with voices that had been broken time and time again during that period, right up to the final whistle and beyond. How many of us had been in Novi Sad to witness that 6–1 mauling by Serbia four years earlier, or watched it on TV? Now here we were, having decimated some of the best teams in Europe, only falling at the penultimate hurdle. What an incredible achievement.

The players came over once again after full time to thank us. 'It's the first semi-final I've ever been involved with, so it is horrible to take, but with hindsight you just have to sit back and look at what we did, the journey we had and what we achieved... To lose to the winners in the semis is no disgrace for any team,' Sam Vokes said, whilst reflecting holistically on the journey Wales have been on. 'From where we were five years ago, to be there in Lyon after that game says everything about how well this team has done; and there's still more to come, I think! A massive thank you has to go the fans – it was a really special moment to put the shirts on saying "Diolch", the fans still singing so loud. Of course we were all a bit gutted, but that moment with the fans, and every moment we spent with the fans, was incredibly special. It was a celebration of how well the tournament went for us, but also our way of saying thank you, because the fans didn't stop singing, even long beyond the final whistle, which you don't often get after losing in the semi-finals of a major tournament.' Ben Davies labelled the post-match celebrations as his proudest moment as a Welshman: 'The biggest moment for me was after we lost to Portugal, standing facing the fans, hearing them sing the national anthem and us players joining in. I've never felt more emotional and proud to be Welsh than at that moment in time. It was as if we had all been on this journey together, and it was coming to an end, but we were both as proud as one another. The players gave everything, as did the fans – that moment will always stick with me.'

Retreating to Dinard for one last night after their semi-final defeat to Portugal, everything began to sink in for Wales' heroes as they enjoyed each other's company – still sore, obviously, after such a tough result – and pondered over what they'd achieved during the last few weeks in the Euros. Spending their last night in France watching les Bleus' semi-final clash versus Germany in Marseille on television, the Welsh were treated like heroes as Dinard was heaving and everyone was out to enjoy the occasion. Discussions had taken place to try and prepare the players for what they'd come back to when they returned to Wales, but as good as that last night away from home would be for Chris Coleman's men, nothing could compare to the homecoming. Coming back after qualification in Zenica, there had been some fans at the airport to greet the squad, but landing in Cardiff this time there were absolutely thousands in the airport alone, really shaking the players and staff and helping them further understand what they'd achieved. But that was nothing to what they would witness once they got into town.

En route into the city on the coach, people were stopping their cars to get out and applaud. There were people standing on roundabouts with flags, clapping, screaming and cheering. There were schoolkids all outside, so excited to see what they thought was one of the best teams in the world. No longer do we have generations of kids who think 'Ah well, Wales, eh?' Now it's all about the Wales team that finished fourth in a major tournament, which the younger generation look up to and are inspired by. They spend their free time in their gardens practising Hal Robson-Kanu's turn, or taking free-kicks like Bale, or running their arses off like Joe Allen or Joe Ledley, imitating Ramsey's touch, anything – kids now wander around in Wales kits again, and love this team. It's all down to this last few years, which have been incredible.

The fans got to give their thanks as the coach arrived at Cardiff Castle, the players then embarking upon an open-top-bus parade ending up in Cardiff

City Stadium, where Wales' summer would finish on the best possible note. 200,000 people apparently lined the streets of Cardiff for the parade – the bus acting as Moses, parting a Red Sea of Wales fans that flowed right from the castle up to the stadium itself, the tide never fading or wavering as red shirts followed the Dragons right through Cardiff on their journey. A walk in the park compared to trips to some of the more isolated cities and countries Welsh fans have visited over the last 58 years, but infinitely more glorious than any journey they'd undertaken before.

'That moment summed it up, that was Wales' tournament – whatever the outcome of the games, there was huge amount of pride for all parties,' Andrew Gwilym said, his own Welsh pride pouring out of him. 'There was a huge amount of pride between everyone – the staff and the players were incredibly proud of the fans, and vice versa, and I think that just shone throughout the whole experience. Welsh football shouldn't be the same after this; it mustn't. Nothing should be the same again after this – nothing. The last five weeks have been an epochal moment in the history of Welsh football. I'm not just talking about the people who maxed out credit cards to go to every game, but the people at home as well – you talk about a connection between a group of players and the people of their country, you look at the response they got back home in Wales. It's just struck a chord with people who are proud to be Welsh. You don't have to support football, they tapped into a national consciousness that goes wider than sport. It's about pride, passion and a shared identity... all of those things came together perfectly for this tournament, and that's why I say things can never be the same again, because it's too big an opportunity, too huge a legacy to let slip through your fingers! Football in Wales could be redefined on the back of what's happened in France, and I hope it is.'

I've got to be honest and say that I'll never have to write anything more difficult than this book, or at least I hope not. To try and encapsulate what this past summer meant to us in mere words is just impossible. I've put 40,000 or so of them together to try and give the tiniest sense of what the events of Euro 2016 meant to us all, and I'm convinced very few of them are right, if any – and I don't think I would have been able to get it right if I'd had a million words to help me. Capturing the emotion, the turmoil, the peaks and troughs of the last few years in *The Dragon Roars Again* – the near-misses, the highs and the devastating lows on and off the pitch – seemed like the biggest challenge in the world at the time, but this has just been something else.

Having spoken to dozens of people for this book, I've asked every single one of them what their standout memory from this past summer was, and the reaction has been unanimous. Whether that be talking to players, to fans, to journalists, to people who've never watched Wales play before but were simply captivated by what our country was doing, I got the same reaction from everyone. Conversations would be flowing, people would be gesticulating about this amazing scene or that amazing scene, Hal Robson-Kanu (who can blame them?) – then I'd ask them, 'So, given all of that, what was the standout? What was the pinnacle?' If these conversations were happening face-to-face you'd think the other person had zoned out, or on the phone you'd be checking they hadn't hung up, then you get the same reaction... a puff of the cheeks, a shrug of the shoulders, heads in people's hands. People just couldn't pick one moment.

As Joe Ledley said, he could have picked 50, but another fantastic individual I spoke to was particularly profound in their summation of this amazing, unbelievable summer full of hair-raising, pinch-yourself moments, and it's his insights that I choose to end this particular journey on. Enter Neil Taylor. 'For me, the time spent with the lads was my favourite thing about the whole experience. Actually there's a conversation we all had at one point in the tournament where we all said maybe we could start our own club football team together! You know, get Gareth to buy Merthyr Tydfil or someone like that, and we could still stay together as a club team. So that would be my lasting memory probably, where we came up with that and every single person was like, 'Yeah, let's do it!' We got on that well as a group of lads – and the staff and the manager – it was just a feeling that we were all part of something together.

'Seeing the looks on everyone's faces: the fans, the players, the staff, that guy who was on camera crying against Russia – we saw him in about three different stadiums, I think – but moments like that made me think what an unbelievable summer it was. We were away from our family and kids for seven weeks, which is really heart-wrenching, but we got on with each other that well and kept each other's spirits up so much, that's what got us through it... Feeling the proudness of the nation, seeing people crying, the unity of the lads – I wish I could just bottle it up and give it to every team I've played for, but there were too many moments for me.

'Even to see the press people – they've been to crap away games in 2007/08/09, games with nothing on them, but for them to be able to experience this as well – it was just nice to see everyone we'd started with to come through to this pinnacle. I've been lucky to come back and play in Wales to see what it's been like, but it's difficult to put something like that into words. Maybe in five to ten years I'll be able to explain it better, but it was such an emotional time.

'Even when my family went on holiday to Sardinia after the tournament, Joe Ledley was there with his wife and kids. I remember his wife saying to my wife how much of a nightmare Joe had been since he'd come back, listening to Lighthouse Family – because that's the song we'd have on the bus before every game, which Gunts would be in charge of, and we kept playing the same songs throughout the tournament. If I hear a song on the radio that we played in the changing room or whatever, then it still makes me think back, and I remember Joe's wife looking at my wife, then my wife looking at me, thinking how I've been a nightmare since I've got home as well.

'That made me think, when Joe's wife said it as well, that all the lads were definitely feeling the same way, that we were devastated it came to an end and how we enjoyed it as much as the fans and everyone else did.'

Also by the author:

'An excellent contribution to Welsh football literature.'
Chris Coleman

The
Dragon
Roars Again

WALES' JOURNEY
TO EURO 2016

#TogetherStronger
FRANCE 2016

JAMIE THOMAS

y Lolfa

£9.99

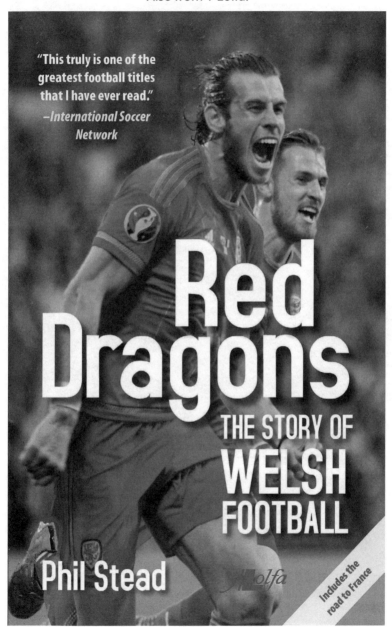

"This truly is one of the greatest football titles that I have ever read."
–*International Soccer Network*

Red Dragons

THE STORY OF WELSH FOOTBALL

Phil Stead

Lolfa

Includes the road to France

£14.95

Ibuprofen sil vous plait!

Dewi Prysor

Teithiau Prysor yn yr Ewros

£9.99

Merci
CYMRU

Dathlu haf bythgofiadwy 2016

Tim Hartley (gol.)

£7.99